PARIS
la ville lumière

Written by:
EVA MARTINEZ AND CATHERINE PINKERT

Photographs by:
PAULE TRUCCHI

editions **ITALCARDS**
bologna - italy

INTRODUCTION

Starting-point of the French roads.

Three-coloured cockade placed on a column in Notre-Dame.

Clovis made Paris, born more than two thousand years ago, the capital of France 1500 years ago. This town, which was to have an exceptional destiny, spread out and grew rich during the centuries, today it is pervaded with historical memories.

Paris was born from an insular village when the Gallic tribe of Parisians settled on an island on the Seine. After the defeat of Vercingetorige (work of Caesar), which took place in Alesia in 51 B.C., the Roman army subjected the village and the whole of Gaul.

The town, called Lutetia, spread onto the left bank around the important North-South commercial axis under the «pax romana». In the 3rd century the retreat of the Roman troups before the barbarian invasions obliged Lutetia to take refuge on the island. In the 5th century the Frankish reign was organized by Clovis, the first Christian king, who made Paris capital in 508. For many centuries afterwards the village prudently entrenched itself in the middle of the river, a natural defense helped by ramparts. The only fortified ways of entry to the island consisted of a small bridge in the south and a large bridge in the north. Even the terrible Vikings, in 885, had to give up after a year of siege. Charlemagne and the Carlovingians left Paris, preferring Aix-la-Chapelle. The town developed on its own, and spread onto the two banks protected by parish walls. The small suburbs which had formed around the bell towers were gradually integrated into the town by the building of town walls by the kings. In fact from the reign of Louis VII (1137-1180), the growing regal authority became more and more responsible for the capital. Louis VII had the Grand Châtelet built. At the beginning of the 12th century, faced with the peril of the English, Philippe Auguste had the first circle of walls built, which confirmed the fact that the University (situated on the left bank) belonged to Paris. From this moment onwards the city expanded with a slow and circular movement starting from the cross formed by the Seine with the north-south axis. At the end of the 14th century, Charles V enlarged the fortifications in order to incorporate some of the suburbs. The circle of walls built by Louis XIII (at the beginning of the 17th century) widened still more towards the west to incorporate more suburbs. Under Louis XIV, the enemy was driven to the frontiers of the reign and so it was possible to transform the walls into avenues which, lined by trees, became pleasant places to walk. Under Louis XVI, Paris reached its present confines with the construction of the «Fermiers Généraux» wall, a customs protection measure. The 60 pavilions built by Ledoux between 1784 and 1787 controlled access to Paris and made the collection of customs dues possible. Very soon afterwards, the unpopularity of this legislative measure gave rise to the saying «le mur murant Paris rend Paris murmurant» (The walls around Paris make Paris mutter). The fall of Napoleon I in 1815 represented a military danger. They decided to build a new fortification, which was finished in 1845. Lastly, in 1860, the confines were fixed

Old Map of the City.

LE PLAN DE LA VILLE, CITE, VNIVERSITE, FAVXBOVRGS DE PARIS AVEC LA DESCRIPTION DE SON ANTIQVITE

Aerial view of the Seine.

Aerial view with panorama of the city.

at the level of the present external «boulevards», which are flanked by the surburban motorway.

If the extension of Paris was controlled by its various circles of walls, what happened to the quality of its urbanistic development? There were basically five periods in which there were doubts of this kind to be taken into consideration. The Gallic-Roman period, which saw the establishment of the north-south axis with the thistle layout. The qualification of the «first urbanistic king» must be given to Henry IV, followed by Louis XIV who, with the help of Colbert, gave superb monuments to the town within the general urbanistic plans. The work of Napoleon I followed these ideas and was mostly completed by Napoleon III. In this way Paris became a modern town, under the guidance of Baron Haussmann: many quarters changed their appearance or were destroyed to make way for wide avenues, parks, perspectives, public buildings, etc.

However, still today the beauty of Paris is derived from its noble unity and by the infinite differences of its quarters, its magnificent views and its narrow, colourful roads. Paris, one and multiple, is, as ever, unforseeable.

THE ÎLE DE LA CITÉ
CRADLE OF THE CAPITAL AND OF FRANCE

Notre-Dame: sculpture.

On the parvis of Notre-Dame's a bronze slab indicates the ideal starting point of all the roads of France: here geography yields to the historical importance of the island where Paris was born. A couple of centuries before Christ some Celtic fishers, the Parisians, settle in an island of the Seine. Lutetia extends along the left bank during the Gaul-Roman period, but the island keeps the essential, that is the imperial palace to the west and a temple to the east.

During the Middle Ages the ancient configuration of the island is confirmed: royal palaces to the west, churches to the east. Although Paris extends on the «continental territory» both to the north and to the south, until the 10th century the island remains the central point to be protected from the assaults of Attila and later of the Normans. Two wooden towers had been erected for this purpose at the entrance of the two bridges, later substituted with the Grand Châtelet (about 1140) and with the Petit Châtelet. Well defended, the island flourishes. Notre-Dame's Cathedral, built in the 12th century, gives rise to the formation of episcopal schools which spread all over Europe. In the musical field, for example, the «École de Notre-Dame» has produced a rich and important repertory; its two masters were Léonin and Pérotin. The palace becomes larger and quite soon encloses among its high walls a gem of the Gothic art at its apogee, the Sainte-Chapelle.

Since Charles V, the kings have deserted their insular residence for the Marais, the Louvre, Vincennes. But the Parliament resides in the palace of the Cité and there undertakes the essential function of the king: that of doing justice. The cathedral becomes archbishopric in 1622. The physiognomy of the western part of the Cité is remarkably modified under the impulse of Henry IV who decides to build the first stone bridge of Paris, the «Pont-Neuf», surrounded by Place Dauphine and Square du Vert-Galant.

Under Napoleon III, baron Haussmann modifies the look of the island destroying its centre. Notre-Dame's parvis is cleared, the streets are enlarged, the Hôtel-Dieu and the barracks (today prefecture of police) rise, the Palace of Justice doubles its surface. We need therefore much imagination if, visiting the island, we want to find again the atmosphere of the narrow and animated alleys which characterized it until the 19th century.

Foreshortening of the Seine with Notre-Dame.

Excursion on the Seine.

NOTRE-DAME'S

Sculpture of Notre-Dame and view.

The cathedral of Paris is the most visited church of France. It is a wonder of the Gothic art, chiefly for its symmetry; Anatole France defined it «as heavy as an elephant, as light as an insect». Built in the lowest point of Paris, it stands out stately at the turn of a street or behind a bridge. From the parvis of Notre-Dame's, remarkably enlarged by baron Haussmann, you can have a very good viewpoint of the façade; the apse and the building as a whole can be admired from the Quai de Montebello. The cathedral itself offers a wonderful view of the city if you climb the 378 steps which lead to its towers.

Construction. This end of the island has been a sacred place at least since the Gaul-Roman period. The pagan temple has been substituted with churches. During the 12th century two churches were built there, one dedicated to Saint-Etienne and the other to Notre-Dame. When Maurice de Sully became bishop of Paris, he decided to build in their place a grand monument to the Virgin. The work began in 1163. The choir was finished just 20 years later, and when Maurice de Sully died, in 1196, the nave was almost finished. The façade was flanked with the towers at the end of the 13th century. Some chapels were then placed among the buttresses, along the side aisles and the choir. As the tribunes obstructed light, they had to be lowered and the windows enlarged. This required the substitution of the simple supporting arches with the flying arches which give the church an elegant and original look. With the construction of the chapels the façades of the transept had remained recessed. Two clever architects, Jean de Chelles and Pierre de Montreuil, extended each transept for a span.

In the 19th century the cathedral is in a serious state of decay. The «Romantic» movement revalues medieval civilization. Besides, Louis-Philippe orders Lassus and Viollet-le-Duc to restore Notre-Dame's completely. The work, which began in 1864, includes the elimination of some added elements, the restoration of the part under the roof, the reconstruction of the statuary, the revision of the stained glass, the reconstruction of the spire, the construction of the sacristy. The methods employed, harshly criticized today, permitted nevertheless to save the building.

History. We are often told that Notre-Dame's summarizes the history of France under its vaults. In 1239, king Saint Louis IX, barefooted, laid there the crown of thorns, which remained there until the unveiling of the Sainte-Chapelle; in 1302 the first States General of the reign, gathered by Philip the Fair, take place there; in 1431 the young king of England Henry VI has himself crowned king of France, and six years later Charles VII has his return on the throne celebrated there with a Te Deum. In 1572 Marguerite of Valois, in Notre-Dame's choir, and the protestant Henry of Navarre, at the church's door, get married; not long after the chiefs of the Ligue swear there their definitive opposition to Henry of Navarre; finally in 1594 the latter, become Henry IV, is present in the choir to the mass for the surrender of Paris. He summarizes his conversion to Catholicism with his famous, laconic sentence «Paris is well worth a mass». In 1660 is here celebra-

Nocturnal view of Notre-Dame.

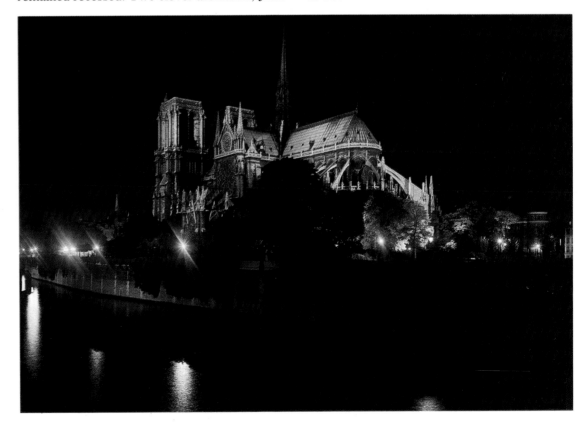

Statue of Charles the Great on the Notre-Dame square.

Autumn at Notre-Dame.

Notre-Dame: façade.

Point de la Tournelle and statue of Sainte Geneviève.

ted, with a Te Deum, the marriage of Louis XIV. Bossuet delivers the celebrated funeral oration of the Grand Condé in 1687. The Revolution renames the cathedral «Temple of Reason», then «Temple of the Supreme Being». On December 2nd 1804, Napoleon is consecrated Emperor in the presence of Pius VII in the church transformed with skilfully arranged hangings; this event is immortalized in David's painting «Le sacre de l'Empereur» (two reproductions of which are at the Louvre and at Fontainebleau). The restored Notre-Dame's has been so far a theatre of the great French events: the marriage of Napoleon III in 1853, the baptism of the Imperial Prince three years later, the national obsequies of great men such as general Foch in 1929, or the poet Paul Claudel in 1955, or general De Gaulle in 1970. Pope John Paul II, in 1980, celebrated the mass on the parvis.

Description of the exterior. The façade, built between 1200 and 1250, is a balanced summary of strength and harmony, and matches the triple vertical division with the three horizontal registers clearly emphasized. At the ground floor the three portals are arranged with intended irregularity. The central one is the most beautiful and the largest; it represents the Last Judgment. The two lower architraves are a reconstruction by Viollet-le-Duc, since Soufflat had suppressed them in 1771 to open a passage for the processional canopy of Louis XV. The portal of the Virgin is surmounted by a pediment. A strange fascination emanates from the characters represented in the upper architrave: the Virgin is crowned by an angel and blessed by Jesus. On their sides are two angels, slightly recessed, who support large candles. The oblique and curved lines which make up the work are characteristic of the «international Gothic» sculpture. Below, a touching sleeping Virgin is represented. The meaning of the anecdote is evident so much so that two apostles have fallen asleep. In the lower architrave, the Ark of the Covenant surrounded by three kings and three prophets. The right portal, called portal of Sainte-Anne, has, in its upper part, an architrave of the church which preceded Notre-Dame's in the 11th century. On the doors, the wrought-iron hinges are masterpieces of medieval art.

On the floor above the portals, the gallery of the kings presents 28 trilobate arcades, each one containing a statue of a king of the Old Testament. It reinforces the horizontal lines of the façade, with a remarkable aesthetic effect. During the revolution these statues were regarded as statues of the kings of France, which caused their destruction; Viollet-le-Duc substituted them with new ones.

The wide rose-window, flanked by two large windows with twin openings, stands out in the centre of the façade. With its 9.60 metres of diameter it is an architectonic challenge.

The plane of the rose-window is surmounted by a gallery of fine small arcades from which the two towers seem to rise, these too with twin openings.

On the north side was once the cloister of the canons. The name of the street (rue du Cloître Notre-Dame) and of the north portal keeps the memory of it. The façade of this transept, as well as the one of the south side, are the work of the architects. J. de Chelles and Pierre de Montreuil. They constitute not only an aesthetic masterpiece, but also a dizzy technical bet: the whole of the rose-window and the flight of windows form an 18-metre-high empty space, where the rose-window alone has a diameter of 13 metres. Under the north portico, the pediment presents in its lower part scenes of the life of the Virgin, in its upper part episodes of the legend of deacon Theophilus, who, after coming to terms with the devil, is saved by the intervention of the Virgin. In the Middle Ages theatrical performances of these scenes sometimes took place on the parvis of Notre-Dame's. In the partition-pillar, the Virgin and Child is a masterpiece of the 13th-century statuary. The canons used to enter their cathedral through the «red door». The pediment is decorated with a relief representing the coronation of Mary — a

Notre-Dame: façade.

Notre-Dame façade: details of the three series; the rose-window (diameter 9.60 metres), the gallery with 28 statues and the entrance portals.

Left portal: the Virgin with the Child.

Notre-Dame: a statue of the façade. From the right: portal of the Virgin, portal of the Judgment, Sainte Anne portal (details).

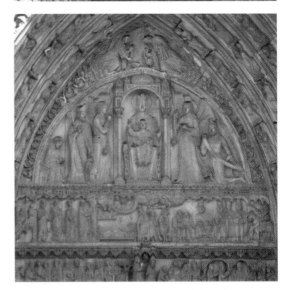

Notre-Dame: the two big large-windows seen from the inside.

work rich in poetry — devoutly framed by the king and the queen: they may be Saint Louis and his wife Marguerite of Provence. In the curvatures, the presence of a carved cordon with dogrose flowers and leaves makes this work likely to be ascribed to Pierre de Montreuil.

The apse is chiefly characterized by the daring beauty of the flying arches (15 metres of light) which seem to crown the head of the building.

The Square Jean XXIII has substituted, since the 19th century, the archbishopric and a quarter of heaped houses.

The spire rises from the cross-vault of the transept. Destroyed during the revolution, it was rebuilt by Viollet-le-Duc.

Interior. The nave, flooded by the changing light of the stained-glass windows, recalls the magnificence of the exterior and strikes him

Page 10-11
Total view of the entrance portals.

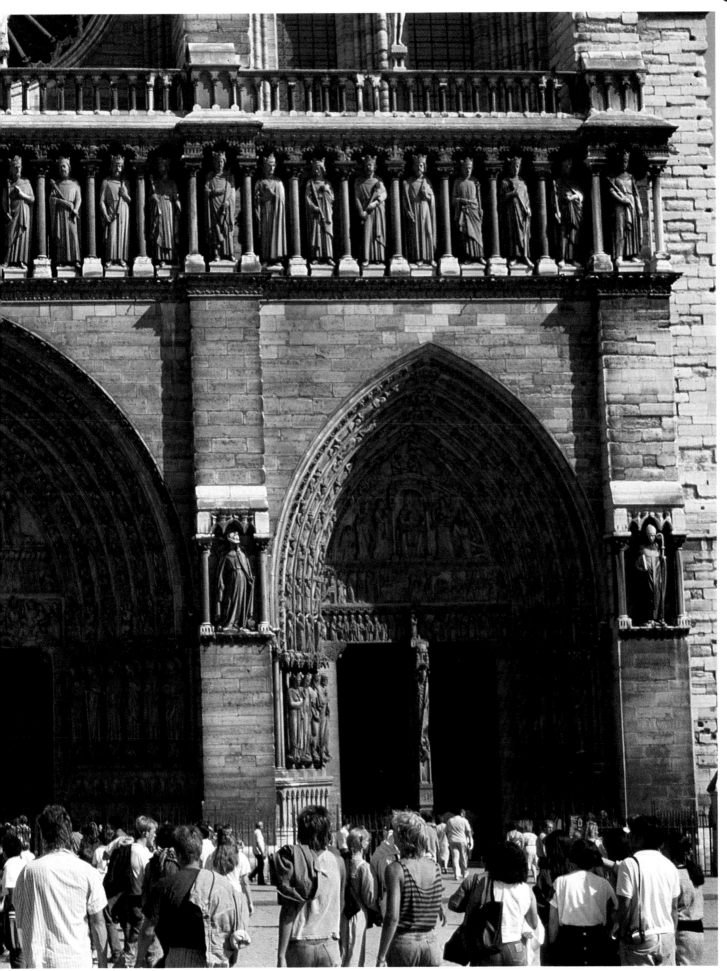

Notre-Dame. The inside: the Pietà.

◀ *Notre-Dame: nave.*

A foreshortening of the Seine with the Law Courts and Pont-au-Change.

who enters with solemnity and grandness. It develops along ten trusses as far as the transept, and rises on three floors. In the 13th century the twin stained-glass windows, less high at that time, were surmounted by oculi; Viollet-le-Duc picked up this solution in the last truss before the transept. The tribune on the 2nd floor and the ogival cross-vaults divided into six parts are a sign of «arcaism» in comparison with the innovations of the rose-windows. The side aisles, double, include seven chapels for each side. The transept is lighted by the north rose-window, almost intact, and by the south rose-window, widely restored.

The choir, whose partition dates back to the 14th century (the bas-reliefs were repainted by Viollet-le-Duc) is classical. As a matter of fact it was redecorated under Louis XIV who in this way wanted to thank the Virgin keeping the vow of his father Louis XIII. The stalls are left today and, behind the high altar, the deposition from the cross by Coysevox flanked by the statues of Louis XIII (by Coustou) and Louis XIV (by Coysevox).

PALAIS DE JUSTICE

In the lower end of the Cité the Roman emperors built a palace, later substituted by that of the Merovingian and Carolingian kings. The Capetians modified it again, especially Saint Louis. He kept there his famous «beds-of-justice», and above all he did an act of piety having the Sainte-Chapelle built near his apartments. Philip the Fair, considering the palace too small to house his judicial, financial and administrative offices, completed the work of Saint Louis with remarkable enlargements. The unveiling took place in 1313. Of this sumptuous palace the three round towers of the Conciergerie, the hall of the guards, the kitchens, the hall of the men at arms remain today. This is a typical example of medieval civil architecture, with its 4 high and long aisles. One morning (February 22nd 1357) the future Charles V (then dauphin) saw his ministers slaughtered under his eyes in his chamber by the Parisian rebels. The dauphin left those places a few months later, substituted by Charles VI. The Valois lived by that time in their palaces of the Marais, the Louvre, Vincennes, the castles of the Loire, and so on, and the Palais de la Cité housed the Parliament, Supreme Court of Justice. The inevitable fires caused the usual damages. But the architectural transformations of the palace date back chiefly to the 19th cen-

The Law Courts.

Rear of the Law Courts.

Law Courts and Sainte Chapelle.

Sainte Chapelle façade.

Law Courts and Sainte Chapelle.

Gate of the Law Courts.

Sainte Chapelle: impressive view of the façade.

tury. Since the revolution (and until today) the palace has been used as «Palais de Justice». In 1840 a new wave of restorations begins, which goes on until the beginning of our century. The fire of the Commune, in 1870, decides for the construction of the wing along Quai des Orfèvres and of the buildings facing Place Dauphine.

Bas-relief of Louis XIV.

*The Sainte-Chapelle:
Interior of the lower part
open to the believers.*

THE SAINTE-CHAPELLE

*Statue of the Virgin with the
Child at the entrance of the
Sainte Chapelle.*

The Sainte-Chapelle, which is now in the courtyard of the Palace of Justice, was built by Saint Louis near the royal apartments with which the upper chapel communicated directly. Louis IX's exemplar piety induced him to purchase reliques, at that time feverishly searched for by christianity. An exceptional opportunity was offered to him: towards 1230 Baldwin II, the Byzantine emperor, was forced to sell the crown of thorns and other reliques of Christ's Passion. Saint Louis purchased them at a very high price, and soon decided to erect an enormous reliquary to protect them adequately in his palace. The realization of the chapel, entrusted to the architect Pierre de Montreuil, required only three years; the consecration took place on April 25th 1248.

The supporting structure of the building is a miracle of lightness: it consists only of a light framework of pillars supported by fragile buttresses. In the place of regular walls rise 15-metre-high glass windows. This daring innovation, unprecedented at the time, carries to extremes the logic of Gothic architecture. According to the by then frequent solution in palatine chapels, this one consists of two floors, the lower part for the staff, the upper chapel reserved to the Grandees of the Reign and linked by means of a corridor to the king's apartments.

A fire seriously damaged the building in the 17th century; the revolution planned its demolition, but finally, under Louis-Philippe, Lassus and Viollet-le-Duc undertook a gigantic restoration.

Interior. After passing under the superimposed arcades, you enter the lower chapel, whose scarce height has induced the director of the work to add two side aisles to the nave. This chapel, ingeniously designed, constitutes a strong basis to the upper part.

This can be reached by means of an interior staircase. Anyone who enters here cannot help feeling an intense aesthetic emotion. The walls are in glass and the glass is wonderful stained glass. This chapel is a «house of light», fully answering the Gothic demands about «mysticism of light» enunciated by Abbé Suger in the 12th century: the light is God, and the faithful, touched by this mediator, participates of the divine essence. The 15 stained-glass windows are really dazzling. Eleven of them represent the Old Testament, one of the nave and four of the apse tell the New Testament and the history of the reliques. Half of the scenes would be original (13th century), but the other half perfectly blends with it thanks to the skilful restoration of the 19th century. The large rose-window, more recent (end of the 15th century), represents the Apocalypse on 86 panels. The statues of the apostles, six of which date back to the 14th century, lean on the pillars, to symbolize perhaps the support of the Church. The elegant whole erected behind the altar has been completely remade by Lassus. The central niche served as a tribune for the reliquary.

Interior of the lower chapel: detail.

Interior of the upper chapel, once communicating with the royal apartments (flats).

The oldest large-windows in Paris: details.

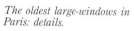

THE CLOCK-TOWER

It is distinguished from the other towers by the rectangular section. It dates back to the half of the 14th century, but it has undergone several restorations, such as the whimsical creation of the battlemented gallery for the rounds (1848). On the façade facing bd. du Palais is, since the epoch of Charles V, a public clock, unique in Paris at that time. At the moment of the restoration under Henry III, Germain Pilon executed the present framing, ornamented with fine sculptures.

Tower of the clock.

THE CONCIERGERIE

Under the revolution. The Conciergerie is a building — of Philip the Fair's time — which flanks Quai de l'Horloge. It owes its name to the «concierge», an important character who, in the Middle Ages, was in charge of administrating the palace. When in the 14th century the palace became the seat of the Parliament, the Conciergerie was gradually transformed into a prison, the first one in Paris. During the revolution it was arranged to contain the maximum number of prisoners. So, for example, between January 1793 and July 1794, 2500 prisoners get out of here to be beheaded in a square of Paris.

The ghost of Queen Marie Antoniette haunts those places: she was imprisoned alone in August 1793, and got out on the following 16th of October to go to the scaffold. Her prison can be visited, but is not recognizable because transformed into a chapel. A corridor divides the prison into two parts: to the north was the «men's department», to the south the «women's department», in whose courtyard the female prisoners washed their cloths. The torture or «question» was performed in the Bonbec tower, from which the name comes.

Conciergerie and Pont-Neuf.

Conciergerie: Gens d'armes hall, architectural complex of rare beauty (1315).

PONT-NEUF

It is the oldest bridge in Paris. Finished in 1604 it completes the arrangement of the west end of the island linking two islets, they too linked by means of Place Dauphine, then under construction. A prestigious work, it was erected under Henry III and Henry IV to requalify the capital and to link comfortably the right bank to the left one, in order to allow the traffic of the «coaches». Moreover, it is the first bridge in Paris in stone and not in wood, and the first (and the only one for a long time) on which no houses were built, which besides permitted to the passers-by to enjoy the sight of the river. A further refined novelty, much appreciated, were the pavements.

The Pont-Neuf soon became then a place of

Equestrian statue of Henry IV.

The «Zouave» of Pont de l'Alma.

Place Dauphine and Pont-Neuf.

Barges at Quai de Conti-Vert Galant Gardens-Pont-Neuf.

attraction privileged by the Parisians and a meeting-place for common people and elegant people. In the recesses arranged along the bridge trainers of animals, puppet showmen, toothdrawers, fools, quacks, chansonniers, and so on found a place. But the most famous attraction was perhaps the **statue of Henry IV,** the first statue planned to be erected to a living king. It was instead eventually installed in 1614, four years after the king's death. The horse is a work by Jean Boulogne and the horseman is a sculpture by Tacca. The whole, broken to pieces and melted in 1792, was substituted by Lemot under Louis XVIII; the bronze used comes possibly from the fusion of the statue of Napoleon that was on the Vendôme column. We are told that the melter secretly slipped an imperial statuette into the king's left arm and some Bonapartist text into the horse.

Place Dauphine.

The department stores «La Samaritaine».

PLACE DAUPHINE

In 1607 the two islets which precede the île de la Cité were united; beyond the Pont-Neuf a beautiful triangular square was built in honour of the Dauphin Louis XIII. Nothing is more fascinating than this combination of stone and bricks conceived by Harlay. The homogeneity and elegance of this square foretell the success of the other royal squares of the 17th century. The destruction of the East side in 1874 unfortunately took away its mysterious appearance.

THE SAMARITAINE

A pump which provided water to the Louvre and the Palais de la Cité was placed near the Pont-Neuf, and was called Samaritaine because there was represented the woman from Samaria who offered water to Christ. The name was taken by the department stores of the Cognacq-Jay family.

THE ÎLE SAINT-LOUIS

Rue Saint-Louis-en-l'Île.

Still in the 16th century three grassy islets preceded the Île de la Cité. In 1614 the Île aux vaches and the Île Notre-Dame were joined, after filling up the channel which separated them. As to the Louviers island, it was linked to the right bank. The new Île Saint-Louis (so named in 1725) was completely built in the 17th century, inside an estate operation directed by the undertaker Marie: it was reclaimed; parcelled, served by two stone bridges (one of them called after the undertaker's name). The architect Le Vau completed the work. Very few modifications later disturbed the original homogeneity, and still today we can see the physiognomy desired by Henry IV and Louis XII. Its fascination, its originality and elegance turn it into one of the walking places preferred by the Parisians. The île can be visited following its «quai», shaded and flanked by noble buildings, on whose façades the numerous plates contribute to evoke their prestigious past, which becomes almost legendary.

At n. 11 of quai de Bourbon we can read *«1643, house of Philippe de Champaigne, painter and waiter of the queen-mother».* At n. 5 of quai d'Anjou we read *«petit hôtel Marigny, built in 1640, inhabited by Rennequin, creator of the machine of Marly».*

The hôtel de Lauzun. Is at n. 17 of quai d'Anjou; it was built by Le Vau in 1656 and purchased by the count of Lauzun when he came out of prison; his imprisonment was requested by Louis XIV to prevent his marriage with the «Grande Mademoiselle», the duchess of Montpensier, cousin of Louis XIII. The count was maybe also secretly visited here by the king's cousin. In the 19th century the young poet

Balcony of the Hôtel de Lauzun.

The Ile Saint Louis and the Ile de la Cité.

Below: Point-Marie and along the Seine.

Charles Baudelaire rented one of the garrets and began here his collection «Les fleurs du Mal». The painter Boissart and the poet Théophile Gautier founded here the «club des Haschis-chins», later joined in by Victor Hugo, Delacroix, Balzac, Daumier. The Commune of Paris has owned it since 1899, and organizes parties here. The solemnity inspired by the fa-çade contrasts with the rich magnificence of the interior, where paintings and sculptures unite in a harmonious exuberance. These apartments are certainly one of the finest 17th-century wholes in Paris.

The last hôtel before rue Saint-Louis en l'Île is the **hôtel Lambert,** which excited Vol-taire's admiration. It was built in 1640 and Le Vau designed a wonderful rotunda which dominates the Seine.

Then the long rue Saint-Louis en l'Île appears, which crosses the whole island, like the main street of a village. Here is concentrated the whole life of the «Louisiens», and it creates a remarkable animation among the several traders. It is also the religious centre, with the **Church of Saint-Louis** en l'Île, whose nave, lined up with the façades of the other buildings, can be noticed only because of the open-work spire and the iron clock. The interior, of Jesuitic style, offers too a fascinating contrast: the walls are covered with gold, marbles, wood, enamels. At n. 51 is the wonderful **hôtel Chenizot.**

But one can also wander at random among the island's alleys, become imbued of its poetry go-ing into the paved courtyards. And not to be despised is the tasting of the famous Bertillon ice-creams, or an evening spent in a wine cel-lar or in one of the attractive restaurants of the island.

Café de Flore.

FAUBOURG SAINT-GERMAIN

The Faubourg Saint-Germain corresponds today to the quarter embraced by the Seine, rue de Varenne, Invalides and rue du Bac. It owes its origin to the extension of the borough grown around the **Abbey of Saint-Germain-des-Prés.** But for a long time a portion of country remains where the buildings gradually rise along the road leading to Versailles, where king Louis XIV and part of the Court live. Then in the 18th century the Marais becomes out-of-date and the Faubourg prevails; numerous and sumptuous hotels for privates rise rapidly. The prestige of the Faubourg is wordly and intellectual at the same time: the banker Samuel Bernard, politicians such as Barras and Talleyrand organize sumptuous parties; M.me du Deffand and M.me Récamier have here their drawing-rooms. In the 19th century the fashion turns to the Champs-Elysées. The transformations operated by this century are limited to the opening of the boulevards Saint-Germain and Raspail.

Rue de Lille, rue de Grenelle, rue de Varenne still recall the prestigious look of the 18th century. All the hotels now seats of embassies and ministries are designed between courtyard and garden, and are noted along the road for the stately door. On rue de Lille we mention the hôtel Turgot, built in the 18th century (n. 121), the hôtel de Seigneulay (n. 80) and the hôtel de Beauharnais (n. 78), built by Boffrand, the hôtel de Salm, built between 1782 and 1787, become Palais de la Légion d'honneur in 1804. In rue de l'Université, n. 15, the hôtel d'Aligre, built at the end of the 17th century; at n. 51 the hôtel Pozzo di Borgo, built in 1707-1708 by Lassurance. On rue Saint-Dominique the older part of the ministry of Defence is visible, consisting of two hotels built by Aubry in 1714 (one was the hôtel de Brienne) and a monastery (n. 14 and 16). At n. 35 the hôtel de Broglie (1724). In rue de Granelle, one following the other, are the hôtel du Châtelet, built by Cherpitel in 1770 (n. 127), the hôtel de Maillebois, built by Delisle-Mansart (n. 102), the hôtel de Bauffremont at n. 87, built between 1720 and 1736, the hôtel d'Avary at n. 85, the grand hôtel d'Estrées built by R. de Cotte for the Duchess of Estrées, in 1713 (n. 79). Rue de Varenne is perhaps the most prestigious. The chief hôtels that are worth mentioning are: at n. 47 the hôtel de Boisgelin, built towards 1787 by Parent; at n. 50 the hôtel de Gallifet, built by Legrand between 1775 and 1796; at n. 57 the hôtel Matignon, a work by J. Courtonne in 1721, now residence of the Prime Minister. At n. 73 Boffrand built the hôtel de Broglie in 1735; at n. 78 the hôtel de Villeroy was erected in 1724.

Panoramic view.

Shop window.

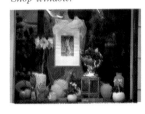

Palais Bourbon seen from Place de la Concorde.

THE PALAIS BOURBON OR ASSEMBLÉE NATIONALE

The Palais Bourbon was originally a habitation built between 1722 and 1728 by Gabriel and Aubert for the Duchess of Bourbon (daughter of Louis XIV and Madame de Montespan). Today however she could not recognize her palace anymore. The contiguous hôtel de Lassay (today Petit Bourbon) is incorporated under Louis XVI, the revolution arranges a meeting-hall in it, Napoleon in 1807 has a façade built by Poyet in front of the buildings facing Place de la Concorde. This façade, with columns, serves as a «pendant» for the «temple» of the Madeleine.

This palace is today the seat of the national assembly. The deputies discuss here in a hemicycle directed by the chairman of the assembly.

THE HÔTEL BIRON OR RODIN MUSEUM

Hôtel Biron seat of the Rodin Museum.

This hôtel, built at the beginning of the 18th century for Peyrenc de Moras, inhabited later by the Duchess of Maine, daughter-in-law of Louis XIV, then purchased by marshal de Biron (from here the name), was placed at Rodin's disposal since 1908 in exchange for the assignment of his works and collections to the State. The museum created in this way was unveiled in 1919.

Built between 1728 and 1731, this residence, for its uniformity, is a good example of «rocaille» architecture, a style of the first half of Louis XV's reign. The king's first architect, Jacques V Gabriel and Jean Aubert direct the work. The north and south façades present roughly the same arrangement: three bodies and three slightly protruding foreparts. On the side of the courtyard the decorations are limited to sculptured masks and shells and to the wrought iron of the balconies. On the side of the garden the scenary is richer. The ornamented corbels which support the balcony are typically «rocaille». The gardens have been rearranged in the 18th-century style. They are inhabited by monumental statues by Rodin. The interior space is structured in a peculiar way. The very rich decoration was remarkably damaged in the 19th century when the religious order — owner

Hôtel Biron seen from the garden.

The Porte de l'Enfer.

«Les Bourgeois de Calais» of Rodin.

Statue of Victor Hugo.

of the place — took away the wooden coverings, associated to sin.

The name of Rodin dominates the sculpture of the end of the 19th century. Independent genius, he opposed the academism which imposed definitively established formulas to the artist. A pupil of Barye, he preserves the mark of Romanticism. He has the sense of the tragic, which we can find in «**La porte de l'enfer**», representing an infinite number of human dramas, in «**Les bourgeois de Calais**» bent under injustice. Passionate poet, Rodin is in love with nature, never sacrifying however his art to an absolute realism, even if his first great work, «L'âgé d'airain» (1875), was accused of being transferred from the living model. This museum reunites the most part of Rodin's works and allows us to know the artist in an exhaustive way. Until 1900 — when, as a part of the Universal Exhibition, a great retrospective

exhibition of his work is organized — he is alternatively flattered or not understood by his contemporaries. In 1864, his bust of «L'homme au nez cassé» is refused at the «Salon des Artistes Français», but in 1880 he receives the important charge of carving «La porte de l'enfer», meant for the future «Musée des Arts Décoratifs» (never built), then «Les bourgeois de Calais» in 1884. In 1889 he exhibits with the impressionist painter Monet, receives the charge for a monument to Victor Hugo (for the Panthéon in Paris), later refused. In 1891 he is ordered a monument to Balzac, this too eventually refused in 1898. After the consecration of his genius at the «Exposition Universelle», «Le penseur» is installed in front of the Panthéon, and a national museum entirely dedicated to Rodin (and to his friends Camille Claudel, Eugène Carrière, and so on) opens for the public in 1919.

The Thinker.

THE ORSAY MUSEUM

At the end of the 19th century, a railway society planned to build a railway station in the area of the destroyed Orsay Palace. Victor Laloux, who obtained the «grand prix» of Rome, directs the work for this gigantic metal structure, camouflaged externally with a stately stone façade and internally with stucco lacunars, a system typical of the beginning of the century. The destination of the station to a different use (some thirty years later) did not mean its demolition: the public opinion exerted a pression to preserve this testimony of 19th-century architecture. In 1975 a project is sketched about transforming it into a museum, which leads in December 1986 to the opening of the Orsay

Museum. Gae Aulenti, Italian architect, is the great protagonist of the transformation of the station into a museographic space. She succeeded in creating a variety of spaces and lights matching that of the exhibited works and pleasant to be seen. The statues are perfectly harmonized with the architectural ambient, perspective effects enhance the canvases. The museum is a link between the Louvre and the Pompidou centre: it is the memory of the second half of the 19th century, from 1848 to 1905. Dedicated not only to painting and sculpture but also to architecture, furniture, glass manufacture, photography, cinema, and so on, this museum expresses the demand for pluridis-

Palais d'Orsay seat of the Museum.

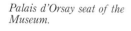

View of Palais d'Orsay.

Hall of the Museum.

Foreshortening of the hall of the sculptures.

ciplinarity, today a major point for European intellectual life. It makes concrete, moreover, another up-to-date aspiration: putting together the academic art of this half of the century and the independent art (chiefly impressionistic), to leave to the public the opportunity of possibly rehabilitating the academism of this period.

The large central lobby extends in the direction of the former railway; exhibition halls surmounted by terraces and communicating with two other floors open around it. Finally, the spaces under the roof are arranged as galleries that exploit the zenith light.

Ground floor. In the lobby the movements which animated sculpture between 1850 and 1870 are present. Romanticism is illustrated by the head of the «Génie de la Patrie» of the «Marseillaise» by Rude, whose expressive power is characteristic of this current. In the opposite sense was developed neoclassicism, here represented by James Pradier — author of a masterpiece of draping: «Sapho» (1852) —, by Eugène Guillaume and P.J. Cavelier. Their cult of Antiquity goes to the extremes in the «Cénotaphe des Gracques», in which E. Guillaume reproduced exactly the Roman funerary art of the 1st century a.D. The Second Empire is dominated by eclecticism, turned towards Italian Renaissance, such as in the elegant «David» by Antonin Mercié (1872) and towards Antiquity, such as in «Trouvaille à Pompei» by Hyppolite Moulin (1863) or in the group «Hébé» by Carrier-Belleuse (1869). Charles Cordier is present with «Le nègre du Soudan» (1857), where the taste for Antiquity, exoticism, magnificence, are characteristic of the adepts of «polychromy». The greatest sculptor of the period, Jean-Baptiste Carpeaux (1827-1875), occupies at Orsay's the place which belongs to him by right and is widely represented, for example, by the original of the famous group of the façade of Opéra Garnier, «La Danse», whose sensuality had nourished so much the polemics of 1869. In the same way, the tormented pyramid-shaped group «Ugolin et ses fils»

The clock of Palais d'Orsay.

La Méditerranée de Maillol. ▶

(1860), executed by the sculptor during his stay at Villa Medici in Rome, roused the violence of Parisian criticism at its arrival in France. One year later, however, in 1862, the State placed in the gardens of the Tuileries a reproduction in bronze (the same of the Orsay's Museum) which became a model for contemporaries. The theme is the death of Ugolino, a character of the Divine Comedy by Dante, who, condemned to die for hunger, ate his four children before.

The spaces surrounding the central area have as a theme painting between 1850 and 1870.

To the right the «classical» painting or «school of design» is represented by the late work of Ingres and his pupils (the «Ingresques») Amaury Duval and Hyppolite Flaudrin. Their opposers, the «romantics», supporters of colour, are exposed very near: their file-leader, Delacroix, the sculptors A. Préault and Barye, the painter Paul Huet as a hinge between the two rival schools, the work of Théodore Chassériau.

On the right side of these halls, other spaces are dedicated to the up-to-date genres of the historical painting and the portraits.

The left part of the central space is consecrated to the universal Daumier, to the painters of Barbizon such as Millet and Théodore Rousseau, to the realists like Hébert. Also remarkably present are Courbet, Puvis de Chavannes, G. Moreau and the impressionists Manet, Degas, Renoir, Monet, Bazille, and so on, preceding 1870. Towards the end of the hall the decorative arts from 1850 to 1880 can be discovered, reconstructions of the Opéra (by Garnier), some architectural and urban transformations by Haussmann, some studies about the architectonic polychromy of Viollet-le-Duc.

The middle floor of the museum houses various collections of the period 1870-1905: the official art of the Third Republic (the painters W.

Bouguereau and B. Constant, the sculptor J.-L. Gérôme), the naturalist movement with Bastien Lepage, Cormon, Dalou, Meunier; but also the major work of the sculptor A. Rodin, looking forward to the 20th century, and of his friends Camille Claudel, Bourdelle and Bartholomé. On the threshold of our century the sculpture of the great Maillol (1861-1941), with the marble piece «La Méditerranée». The symbolist current, with Eugène Carrière, Henri Martin, tries to express dream in opposition to realism and impressionism. The «Art Nouveau» is widely represented and shows to what extent this end of the century desidered the unheard-of, the original both in architecture and in furnishing.

In the upper corridors, under a zenithal light, wide surveys of the impressionistic and neoimpressionistic movements can be admired.

Outside official art, impressionism develops in France during the last third of the century. In the sphere of painting it links representation to the idea of instantaneity and privileges slight touches, light and dissociated colours. This true pictorial revolution is led by a group of chiefly French artists: around Monet, Renoir, Pissarro, Sisley, Berthe Morisot, Van Gogh, Cézanne, Guillaumin, Degas and others unite. In this museum the original contribution of each of them can be singled out thanks to the quantity and quality of the collections. We can mention «La gare Saint-Lazare» by Monet, seven canvases of which exist, «Le bal du Moulin de la galette» painted by Renoir on Montmartre hill, «L'absinthe», in which Degas interprets space in a totally new way, a group of dancers sculptured by the latter, series of «meules» and «cathédrales de Rouen» where Monet studied light in a particular way, some reconstructions of Giverny (Monet's house) with the «Numphéas» or the «Pont japonais», the fluid colour of: «La chambre de Van Gogh à Arles» «pommes et oranges», where Cézanne treats still life in a new way.

The Neoimpressionists are all present too: the divisionists Seurat, Signac, Cross; the Nabis, with Bonnard, Vieillard, Denis Valloton.

Three halls, dominated by Degas and Redon, are dedicated to the technique of pastel.

Carpeaux: «La danse».

The impressionism

The Museum provides wide space for this pictorial art which displayed the signs of becoming a movement in France in the years following the deep crisis of the Commune. It marked the break off against the academical late-romantic, conventional painting, proposing a new way of painting which could interpret life and the world: a straight way, rich of freshness and candour in which emotion overwhelms technical elaboration, so as to make an imperfect sketch, but alive and sincere, become more important than a painting carried out using all the skill expedients. The main figures of the impressionism were Manet, Monet, Renoir, Degas, Sisley,

Pissarro, Cézanne, Seurat. The word «impressionism» derives from the title (Impression: Soleil levant) of a Monet's painting, exposed in Paris in 1874.

▲ Claude Monet (1840-1926) «Poppy Fields»

After having started as a caricaturist, his friend Eugène Boudin initiated him in the painting of landscapes from life and persuaded him to continue his studies in Paris. After various experiences he approached Manet's art and so he started new researches into lightness and colour, impressions of ambient and suggestions of landscape, becoming the most genuine representative of the French impressionist painting. He had a quivering and estatic vision of nature, like in the famous cycles about one subject (the Rouen Cathedral) reproduced in different hours of the day.

◄ Pierre-Auguste Renoir (1841-1919) «Moulin de la Galette»

First-rate exponent among the impressionist painters. After various experiences in the field of painting, in 1872, together with Monet, he adopted the impressionist technique, creating his renowned, vaporous, magic nudes. Skilful colour user, Renoir used clear and joyous tonalities, especially pink and light-blue, led on canvas with the utmost delicacy and sprinkled with light.

◄ Paul Gauguin (1848-1903) «Paysannes bretonnes»

George Seurat (1859-1891) «The Circus»

Leader of the group of the post-impressionists, at first interested in landscape painting and attracted by impressionism, he wanted to apply to his art the results of the scientific researches realized in that period in the field of optics and physics. He was the first one to adopt the technique of the divisionism or «Pointillisme» consisting in covering the whole surface of the canvas with coloured points obtaining effects of extreme lightness and brightness. He is a painter who reached a high artistic reputation far from the impressionist techniques.

Vincent Van Gogh (1853-1890) *«La chambre de Vincent en Arles»*

After many experiences practised in Holland (teacher, salesman, preacher) about in 1881 Van Gogh began to show interest in painting, turning his attention at first to Daumier, Couber, Milbet, then he moved to Paris meeting Gauguin, Seurat and Toulouse-Lautrec, learning from the impressionist school the taste for a lively chromatism, which we discover in the numerous self-portraits and its still-lifes. He was an outstanding artist thanks to the life charge we find in his paintings which is displayed not only by colours but also by lines and materials, reaching the highest expressive outcomes. That's why Van Gogh is considered one of the great masters of modern painting.

this way Cézanne, going through this research, not only excelled the impressionism itself, but also built the bases for a further development of the modern pictorial art becoming, in a certain way, the forerunner and the beginner of the cubist movement.

Alfred Sisley (1839-1899) *«La neige à Louveciennes»*

He was English, but he grew and began his activity in France. School-fellow of Monet. Renoir, Bazille, but mainly in touch with Monet, he devoted himself to painting landscapes from life. Exponent of the impressionist movement, strictly bound up with the English artistic tradition, in particular with the landscape painting of the end of the 18th century, he drew from it that particular brightness which is the distinctive mark of his style.

Paul Cézanne (1839-1906) *«Apples and oranges»*

Delacroix and Decoubert were the artists who chiefly influenced the juvenile productions of the artist, in the years 1865-1869. The impressionism and his friend Pissarro were fundamental for his further artistic development. Cézanne concentrated his efforts on the colour as determinant element of the structure, enriching it with a range of tunes, newer and clearer than before, using these means for giving his figures, objects, landscapes, a consistency of volumes. By painting landscapes he wants to pursue abstract geometrical forms: cones, cubes, spheres, not anymore the poetry of a sunset or the thrill of a dusty afternoon, as he wrote in 1904. In

Berthe Morisot (1841-1895) «*Le Berceau*»

Disciple of Guichard and Corot, she was strongly influenced by Manet, being his sister-in-law, becoming so an interesting exponent of the impressionistic school. She was very skilful in portraits and open-air landscapes which she painted with grace and sensibility.

Paul Gauguin (1848- ▶ 1903) «*White horse*»

He began painting drawing influence from the impressionists, but soon he left them to create his own personality: in argument with the naturalism he set the creation of reality against the mere reproduction of it. He realized this plan especially through unreal colouring, rich of yellow, violet, indigo, emerald green; he painted landscapes with red fields and blue trees, taking care not to reproduce nature, but to create chromatic complexes fit for providing emotions. A character of his painting is also the linearism reminding the Italian primitives, and a frequent symbolism.

«Shakespeare and Co», la Bûcherie.

QUARTIER SAINT-GERMAIN-DES-PRÉS

This old quarter of Paris is situated on the ex property of the Saint-Germain abbey. It has maintained its antique appearance although it has remained a very lively centre.

Its tangle of picturesque streets lead us to discover new aspects of the quarter, although the opening of bd. Saint-Germain has slightly changed its shape.

*In **place Saint-André-des-Arts** we already find ourselves immersed in this special atmosphere: it is a small square — its name is that of the church which preceeded it — surrounded by ancient houses and occupied by the «terrasses» of open air cafés from the first rays of sunlight every day.*

*At the end of the 19th century, Saint-Germain-des-Prés became a meeting place for intellectuals. The cafés with famous names, such as «**Le Flore**», «**Les deux Magots**», «**La Brasserie Lipp**», have been meeting places for many writers and artists.*

*There were many publishers of literary works here, some still remain with their wooden shop windows, such as that of «**Shakespeare and Co.**».*

Hidden in the corners you can find the small shops of the antiquarians, the «cabaret» in the «cantine» or night clubs which have taken the place of small theatres.

Place (square) Saint André des Arts.

Medicine School.

ÉCOLE DE MÉDECINE

At the beginning it was the area of the «Académie Royale de Chirurgie» (the Royal Academy of Surgery), it was suppressed at the time of the revolution and reappeared in 1794 with the name of «École de Santé», which brought together both doctors and surgeons.

It was built in the place of the ex church of Saint-Côme and Saint-Damien (the patron saints of doctors) and of the «Collège de Bourgogne», in neogreek style by the architect Gondoin.

In the interior is a fountain, a columned courtyard decorated with a beautiful statue of Bichat, work of David d'Angers.

ÉGLISE DE SAINT.-GERMAIN-DES-PRÉS

Church of Saint-Germain-des-Prés.

The attraction of this church is due both to its architectural style and to its history: it is the oldest church in Paris and maintains traces of its past.

It is on the site where there was once the temple of Isis and the statue of the Egyptian godess, which disappeared under the rule of Clovis.

The first church was built in 543 by Childret I, Clovis' son, in order to preserve a fragment of the Holy Cross and a piece of Saint-Vincent's tunic, brought from Spain.

Here the tombs of the Merovingian kings were also placed.

The church takes its name from Saint-Germain, bishop of Paris, who died in 576 and is buried there.

In the 8th century it became known as Saint-Germain-des-Prés due to the fields which surrounded it.

It became the home of a flourishing Benedectine community (which kept itself apart from civil affairs and was dependant only on the pope).

Church of Saint-Germain-des-Prés.

During the Norman invasion it was consider-

ably damaged and so it was demolished and in its place a romanesque church was built, of which the bell tower preceeded by an atrium remains.

Due to the increasing number of monks, a larger choir was built soon afterwards and was consecrated by Pope Alexander III in 1163.

The new construction of the monastery buildings was started in the 13th century.

The abbey chapel, built between 1245 and 1255 by Pierre de Montreuil, was considered a masterpiece of the Middle Ages. Unfortunately it was destroyed in 1802. However some of the remains are preserved in the square on the left of the church and in the gardens of the Cluny Museum.

After loosing its severity under their decadent regime of the commendatory monks, it joined the austere benedectine congregation of Saint Maur in 1631. It became then an intellectual centre which collected works by scholars like Félibien, Mabillon and Bernard de Montfaucon.

The revolution did not spare it either. The monastic buildings were turned into a warehouse and a prison and it was here that, in September 1792, a cruel massacre occurred in which a number of priests and aristocrats were killed.

Later on the church was transformed into a salpetre factory and that caused the loss of the royal tombs.

Its restauration, however, was initiated in 1819, and on that occasion it was necessary to demolish the two towers of the transept. Further restaurations were carried out by Baltard in 1843: he replaced the capitals of the nave and decorated those the nave and the choir with paintings and gildings.

The frescoes displaied above the portico represent scenes from the Gospel and from the Old Testament and were painted by Hyppolite Flandrin, a pupil of Ingres.

The massive bell tower is still standing there with its atrium today (one of the oldest in France), in memory of the abbey church, in spite of the fact that its last floor was rebuilt in the 12th century restored in the 19th century and crowned by a modern spire.

At the end of the 16th century the apse was supported by semi circular pointed arches — a great novelty — of the same period as those of

Place Fürstenberg.

Notre-Dame. However the church is not very large (65 m long, 21 m wide and 19 m high), it is only half the size of Notre-Dame.

Going through the 17th century atrium you can see a graceful doorway decorated with a wrought iron grating of 1958, by Subes who is also responsible for the gratings around the choir.

Two square side chapels open onto the cloister, these were reconstructed in 1960 in the style of the ancient chapel of Saint-Syphorien.

Until 1646 the nave and the transept were covered by a wooden ceiling which narrowed the gothic vault (the tall arches are modern).

The four naved choir terminates in a hemicycle.

The arcade supported wooden balustrades which in the 17th century were tranformed into three mullioned windows, with small marble columns of the Merovingian age.

In the wings of the transept you can find the

Below: Place Fürstenberg and a typical lane of this quarter.

tomb of king J. Casimiro of Poland, a work by the Marcy brothers and the statue of Saint-Francis Saverio, a Guillaume Coustou's work. In the entrance is the statue of Notre-Dame-de-la-Consolation, in marble of the 15th century which is always surrounded by candles.

On the southern façade is the doorway of Saint-Marguerite which opens onto the small garden of bd. Saint-Germain.

The tradition is that the abbey had the belt with which Saint-Marguerite tied up the dragon.

PALAIS ABBATIAL

The Abbey Palace rises to the east of the church of Saint-Germain-des-Prés and receives various civilian and parish functions.

It was built by Guillaume Marchand at the request of cardinal Bourbon and was then enlarged by cardinal Fürstenberg in 1691; he also opened a passageway into a courtyard, which today corresponds to rue and place Fürstenberg.

It is a stone and brick building, original in its time for its tall windows, its different colours (bricks, stone and bluish slating on the roof) and the absence of sculptures.

PLACE FÜRSTENBERG

This is certainly one of the most graceful squares in Paris, where the passer-by is won over by the fascination of the trees and the white spherical lamps.

At number 6 the painter Delacroix had his atelier.

MARCHÉ SAINT-GERMAIN

Today the market shares with the Hôtel des Examens, the esplanade of the ex exhibition of Saint-Germain. The buildings of the exhibition were built in the gardens of the Saint-Germain-des-Prés abbey: this exhibition was an annual event of great economical importance.

It is said that king Henry IV fell into debt there in 1607 for 300 «scudi».

It was suppressed by the revolution; in 1818 the market took its place.

COUR DE ROHAN

This courtyard, formed by a succession of three small courtyards, has maintained its picturesque appearance. Its name is derived from an alteration of the name of the city of Rouen.

In fact, at the beginning of the XVIth century, the Hôtel in renaissance style was built by the archbishops of Rouen and is still partly visible in the second courtyard. Here it is also possible to see the «pas de mule», the last in Paris, which was used to mount horses.

The first courtyard preserves the remains of the well-curb with small statues of an old well surmounted by a pulley.

The third courtyard gives on to the «cour de commerce Saint-André» of 1791, when a breach was opened in the walls by Philippe Auguste.

The Brasserie (beer pub or bar) Lipp.

BRASSERIE LIPP

It is on the corner ot place Saint-Germain-des-Prés and a meeting place which is especially appreciated by writers and famous people.

During the twenties it was the refuge of André Gide and of the authors of the «Nouvelle Revue Française».

CAFÉ DES DEUX MAGOTS

This has taken its name from the ancient hosiery shop which preceeded it: the owner had given it this name following the success of the theatrical opera «Les Deux Magots de Chine», by Charles-Auguste Séverin. In fact it is still possible to see the two Chinese «Magots» (grotesque statues from the far east) on the sides of the pillars.

As from the beginning of the century it has seen a great number of painters, sculptors, academicians cadets and writers there: Jean-Paul Sartre and Simone de Beauvoir went to work there.

In 1933 the «des Deux Magots» prize awarded to new writers was created. The first prizewinner was Raymond Queneau.

Café des deux Magots.

Rue Mouffetard, the market.

THE PONT DES ARTS

This could not have been given a better name: in fact the bridge of Art connects two marvellous palaces, the Louvre and the Institut de France.

It was built in 1804 under Napoleon and is the forerunner of architecture in open metal; in fact it is the first metal bridge.

It is reserved for pedestrians and offers them an exceptional view of the Île de la Cité, where the towers and spire of Notre-Dame are outlined against the sky.

This magical walk is often made cheerful by musicians and fascinated numerous poets and artists.

INSTITUT DE FRANCE

Here rises the famous dome, so much aimed for by men of letters for what it symbolizes. However the «Institut» does not only include the «Académie Française» (created by Richelieu), where the election of a new member is a national event; but it also includes the «Académies des Inscriptions et des Belles Lettres, des Sciences, des Beaux-Arts et des Sciences Politiques et Morales».

In 1661, few days before his death, Cardinal Mazarino left 2 million francs for the building of a college for 60 pupils from provinces connected with France under his ministry: Piedmont, Alsatia, Artois and Roussillon.

Therefore Le Vaun, appointed by Colbert, started the construction of the college of the four nations, which opened its doors in 1688.

During the revolution it was closed and used as a prison and then as the «École des Beaux Arts» (School of Fine Arts).

The «Institut de France», a revolutionary creation which united the ancient royal academies and the classes of Moral and Political Science, wanted to register discoveries and to contribute to the improvement of the Arts and Sciences. At that time its seat was in the Louvre.

In 1805, Napoleon assigned it to the ex college of the four nations.

Institut de France, particular views.

On the left, from above: Pont des Arts and Institut de France.

This majestic building, connected to the Louvre by the Pont des Arts, greatly represents French architecture of the century, due to its symmetry around the chapel. This, centre of the composition, is arranged by two curved wings, with two series of columns which end in square pavilions with a solid appearance. This is surmounted by the famous dome where the Mazarino coats of arms are sculptured on the tambours. Under this dome the presentation of new members is carried out and here you can also find the tomb of Mazarino made by Coysevox in 1689.

To the right of the garden is the hall of Solemn Sessions, to the left is the Mazarino library.

ÉCOLE DES BEAUX ARTS

This is to be found on the site of the ex monastery of the Augustines, today only the chapel and the cloister remain.

The latter was used as the «Musée des monuments français» (Museum of French Monuments) by the archaeologist Alexandre Lenoir, who dedicated his whole life to saving the works of art of monuments devastated during the revolution.

Two views of the Ecole des Beaux-Arts (school of arts).

This museum was scattered in 1816 and gave its place to the construction of the «École des Beaux Arts», work of Debret and Duban. Short-

ly afterwards the school was enlarged annexing other buildings including the Hôtel de Conti and the Hôtel de la Brazinière.

The chapel, built in 1617, has a high renaissance arcade, which decorates the doorway of the Anet castle, this is a work by Lenoir. Behind the chapel is the «Chapelle des Louanges».

In the second courtyard is the library in Italian style.

The arcade of the «du Mûrier» courtyard, of a Florentine fascination, occupies the area of the ex cloister of the monastery.

In the courtyards and in the gardens you can admire numerous remains of the Saint-Denis basilica, ancient castles or hotels.

The «École des Beaux Arts», a museum, wanted to surround its students with an ambient which would inspire them.

THE SAINT-SULPICE QUARTER - LUXEMBOURG

This is a heterogeneous complex which includes various quarters, each one characterized by its own main monument: **Théâtre de l'Odéon,** *the* **church of Saint-Sulpice,** *the Luxembourg Palace and Park, the* **Observatory.**

These quarters, divided between houses of the gentry and parks or gardens, have, however, a peaceful atmosphere, which is much appreciated by the passer-by.

Saint-Sulpice seen from the Luxembourg.

ÉGLISE SAINT-SULPICE

This church was founded in the 12th century from the abbey of Saint-Germain-des-Prés in order to deal with the great increase of the faithful; it was then enlarged and rebuilt in the 17th and 18th century; for this reason the choir is older than the façade by about a century and a half. The façade was built following the design by the Florentine Servandoni, who won the competition organized for this purpose. Meissonnier's project, which was discarded, was extremely complex. With this façade, Servandoni, who certainly lacked nothing in immagination as far as Meissonnier is concerned, showed, with this façade, his ability of classic simplicity. The double arcades and the columns used as a support for the trabeations, were a novelty at the time of Louis XV. This architectural conception prefigures the succeeding classification research.

The two towers are different and the one on the left is incomplete. Differing from the façade, the body of the building is of beautiful proportions in a Greek-Roman style, supported by buttresses which seem as if they were upturned corbels, ending in the east with the dome of the chapel of the Virgin. The southern façade of the transept is an example of the «Jesuit» design: the two superimposed sequences are framed by two small wings.

The interior: the most noteworthy part is perhaps the chapel of the Virgin, built behind the choir. Servandoni has expressed the taste of his age with the theatrical prospective and lighting effects; in fact the chapel is illuminated by windows which are invisible from the nave. The Virgin and Child is by the sculptor Pigalle, the mural paintings by Van Loo and the fresco of the dome by Lemoyne.

Church of Saint-Sulpice.

Saint-Sulpice: the fountain.

PALAIS DU LUXEMBOURG

Today this is the seat of the senate, one of the assemblies which form the French Government, but its origins are very different.

The construction of the palace was decided by Maria de Medici who did not feel at home in the Louvre after the death of Henry IV and preferred to live in a palace which reminded that of her Tuscan home.

Salomon Brosse built this palace in 1615 in the place of the Hôtel du Duc de Luxembourg, inspired by the Pitti Palace. However, in spite of the Italian style ashlar, the ringed columns and the Tuscan capitals, the Palace is more like a Parisian habitation with its courtyards and garden. It was officially called Palais Médicis but the Parisians did not decide to call it anything other than Palais du Luxembourg.

The Petit Luxembourg, connected to the Palace by a corridor, was left to Cardinal Richelieu who abandoned it to go and live in the Palais Cardinal. Today it has become residence of the President of the Senate. L'Orangerie, built in 1850 without much originality, was seat of the Musée du Luxembourg which became the embryo of the Musée National d'Art Moderne (National Museum of Modern Art).

In 1621 Rubens decorated an entire gallery with 24 paintings which represented the life of Maria de Medici in an allegorical sense. In 1815 they were transferred to the Louvre, where they constitute the Galérie Médicis.

Later Chalgrin restructured the interior of the

The Palace and the gardens of the Luxembourg.

Palace, constructing in particular the magnificent hall of honour, enframed by lions at rest, which leads to the Galérie des Rubens.

The dome of the library was decorated by Delacroix with marvellous paintings representing limbo.

Half way through the 19th century, Alphonse de Gisors transformed the Palace keeping its original style. He added a protruding façade and two corner pavilions to the garden side.

In 1970 the presence of the Senate made a modernization of the Galeries necessary.

This Palace has been used for many activities: it was the property of the Royal Family until the revolution when it took on a less important role because it became the Maison Nationale de Sûreté (Civil Protection). In the end it became seat of many different Parliamentary assemblies: the Directory, (at the end of the 18th century), the Consulate and the Senate installed there by Napoleon Bonaparte.

JARDIN DU LUXEMBOURG

The Panthéon seen from the gardens of the Luxembourg

«A delightful place, a solitary refuge
Open nevertheless in the evening and morning
The schoolboy with his book in hand
The dreamer with his laziness
The lover with his loved one
Entered there, as if into Paradise».

Alfred de Musset

This heaven of green and peace is imbued from time to time by the students' atmosphere of the Latin Quarter or by the gravity of the surroundings of Saint-Sulpice.

There are many who wander idly in the woods, breathing the romantic atmosphere which is exhaled by this changing park with many harmonious aspects.

It is the reign of children: miniature sailing boats challenge each other to regattas on the hexagonal pool, there is a puppet theatre (created in 1881), donkey rides, round-abouts with wooden horses, everything is magical. Players of bowls, lawn tennis or croquet find happiness there.

The park is arranged according to the axis of the Palace, although this is not in the centre, but at an extremity of the park. It is also true that when it was created, the land was limited by the property of the Chartreux which gave it a long narrow aspect limiting its perspective with the Observatoire fountain.

In the beginning the gardens were organized by Nicolas Descamps, then by J. Boyceau in a pure French style: the immense esplanade is interrupted at the centre by a hexagonal pool surrounded by terraces. The pool was enlarged in 1836 and is flanked by two columns dominated by statues.

On both sides of the axis, woods give a «wilder» appearance to the park.

It was not until the revolution that the Char-treux property was annexed to the Luxembourg gardens, in a way that at last the perspective arrived at the Observatoire fountain.

The Chartreux agricultural tradition continued with the nursery, this is on one side of rue d'Assas, created by Daubenton, and includes most species of French trees. Bee-keeping, which is often ignored, has an important place here, with about twenty bee-hives.

The orchard of the Chartreux family, which skirts rue Guynemer and rue Auguste Comte, was redesigned in English style in the 19th century according to the fashion of the age.

During the reign of Louis-Philippe the gardens were gradually decorated with an impressive number of statues, which are now a museum on their own behalf. The statues of the Queens of France and of famous women face the basin of the terraces. Among this multitude of statues the power of Delacroix's monument must be mentioned, it is a work of Dalou, as the Beethoven's bust among the flower-beds, near the amazing work of Pierre Roche «L'effort» (the effort), exploited by the natural scenery on a sandstone rock.

FONTAINE MÉDICIS. The de Medici fountain was only a nymphaea at the beginning; it was moved half way through the 19th century, when the rue de Médicis was opened.

Nowadays it is hidden under tall plane trees at the extremity of a small basin.

Its freshness is one of the most romantic notes in the Luxembourg gardens.

It is characterized by an Italian style ashlar; the part of the garden which gives onto rue de Médicis, is decorated with a bass-relief by Achille Valois (1807) which comes from an ex fountain: it represents Leda and the swan.

Fontaine des Médicis.

Fontaine des Médicis: detail.

The Panthéon seen from the Luxembourg.

In the central niche there is a work by Auguste Ottin (1863): the cyclops Polyphemus (in bronze) who is threatening Galatea and the shepherd Aci (in marble).

OBSERVATOIRE

Since 1919 it has been the seat of the «Bureau International de l'Heure» (International Hour Office), which gives out the universal timetables.

The famous speaking clock is exact thanks to the precision, which almost beats a millionth of a second, of clocks situated in cellars of 28 m depth, where the constant temperature is of 11°86.

On the 21st June, the day of the summer solstice, Colbert and Louis XIV started work (only finished in 1672) following a plan by Claude Perrault. He did not want to break the lines of the construction and for this reason the dome and the wings were only added during the reign of Louis-Philippe.

The Cassini family of Italian astronomers continued to work there until the second half of the 19th century.

Worthy of note in the research carried out by the Observatory are the following: *the calculation of the true dimensions of the solar system, the exact determination of the longitudes, the speed of propagation of light.*

The Observatoire is a one floor rectangular building and its façades correspond exactly to the cardinal points of the compass. The south of Paris goes through the centre of the construction.

The northern façade is flanked by two octagonal towers. The only decoration is formed by two bass-reliefs showing scientific instruments.

The building was realized without using either iron or wood in order to avoid magnetic interferences and also to reduce the risk of fire. For the same reason the roof of the main hall is vaulted.

These rooms mainly contain ancient astrological instruments and documents on the history of its construction.

FONTAINE DE L'OBSERVATOIRE.
The fountain of the Observatory is the work of three famous sculptors: Davioud, Carpeaux and Frémier. It symbolizes four of the five parts of the world (the oceans are not represented for symmetrical reasons).

At the top is the work of Carpeaux: a stone sphere is lead in a kind of dance by four figures of women who represent the different races.

The «four parts of the world» are evidenced by the eight fiery horses which prance around the pedestal, work of Davioud, as are the tortoises and dolphins by the animal sculptor Frémier.

Observatoire (observatory): the fountain.

THE MONTAGNE SAINTE-GENEVIÈVE Core of the latin quarter

During the period of peace following the wars with the Romans, Paris extended beyond the Île de la Cité, mostly on the hill (later called Montagne Sainte-Geneviève), protected from floods. The Roman-planned city rose around the «cardo» (now rue Saint-Jacques), main north-to-south street towards Soissons and Orléans. Though Lutetia is not very important, the main Roman public buildings are placed here in order to romanize the Gauls: the forum, where is now the Panthéon, an amphitheatre, of which some remains are extant, three thermal establishments, one of which has partially kept until today.

*The invasions push the Parisians towards the fortress-island of the Cité. During the first millennium the great **abbeys of Saint-Germain-des-Prés** and **Sainte-Geneviève,** which rise on the right bank, are poles of attraction. But we have to wait until the 12th century to see the real small villages (the «bourgs»), whose name comes from that of the protector abbey. To the two latter abbeys that of Saint-Victor has been added, where Abélard and Guillaume de Champeaux founded a theology school. They start in this way a very important phenomenon: the teachers and pupils who want to get free of the episcopal control of the school of Notre-Dame leave the Île de la Cité and settle along the left bank.*

Perspective view: in the background the Panthéon.

These «bourgs» however did not belong to Paris. Philippe Auguste, «the first Parisian king» would ratify, at the beginning of the 13th century, the scholastic and urban phenomena. He grants the guilds of teachers and students the possibility of being independent from the bishop of the Cité: this «university» of Paris, the first in France, is under the direct control of the king and the pope. In 1215 the bishop and the clergy of the left bank are dismissed from their right of conferring the qualification to teaching, by then a privilege of the teachers. As for urbanization, its development is proved by the necessity of creating for the faithful parish churches near the monastic sanctuaries: Saint-Nicolas-du-Chardonnet, Saint-Etienne-du-Mont, Saint-Sulpice. And above all, Philippe Auguste has a circle of walls built from the Seine to the top of the Montagne Sainte-Geneviève; its layout marks still today the boundaries of the Latin Quarter, so called because until the revolution teachers and students used to speak Latin. Such boundaries are constituted by rue des Fossés Saint-Bernard, rue du Cardinal Lemoine, rue de l'Estrapade, rue des Fossés Saint-Jacques, rue Monsieur le Prince, rue de l'Ancienne Comédie and rue Mazarine.

At the two ends, on the Seine, the defensive system was completed in the 19th century with the Tour de Nesles and the castle of the Tournelle. Under Louis XIV the circle of walls was abandoned and the ditches were filled up; it became then possible to open the above mentioned streets. Baron Haussmann opens towards 1860 rue des Écoles, bd. Saint-Michel and bd. Saint-Germain. But still today the Latin Quarter partly maintains its medieval physiognomy and students' atmosphere.

CLUNY'S MUSEUM

Hôtel de Cluny: detail.

On the right: Hôtel des Abbés de Cluny, seat of the Museum.

Cluny Museum. Hall of tapestries: Lady with the unicorn (young woman with animals in the background strewn with flowers). On the right: façade of the Collège de France.

At the foot of the mountain, the «thermes du Nord» are now included in Cluny's Museum. They were, at the beginning of the century, a superb palace, one third of which remains today. The gymnasia can be seen from bd. Saint-Germain, the tepidarium and the calidarium from bd. Saint-Michel. But the most remarkable remains are inside the museum: above all, the frigidarium, or hall of the cold baths, with daring cross vaults, prow-shaped corbels and brick beds. This hall is the only one in Gaul which has maintained its vaults.

In late Middle Ages the ruins were inhabited. Then, between 1485 and 1510, Jacques d'Amboise, the abbot of Cluny, had the present building built on the eastern part of the ancient monument. It is a civil habitation, Parisian residence of this great abbot, brother of cardinal d'Amboise (minister of Louis XII). The architectural style still belongs to the Gothic period, in this end of century so refractory to Italian influence. A flowery balustrade follows the rounds. But the elements of military architecture, such as the entrance, the battlement, the small towers, are here merely decorative. The spirit of the building is already Renaissance, for example in its «U» shape between courtyard and garden. The chapel is directly linked to the first-floor apartments. The director of work gave it a harmonious impetus endowing it with a slender central pillar which opens in a graceful group of flamboyant small arcades.

With the revolution the hotel became national property. The first floor was soon rented to Alexandre du Sommerard, lover of the Middle Ages and of the Renaissance, who arranged there his collections. They constituted the core of the present museum, which was opened in 1844.

The museum counts collections of the Gaul-Roman period and above all of the Middle Ages, which are richly represented by sculptures, goldsmith's wares, stained glass, paintings, tapestries. There are exhibited important numerous tapestries called «millefleurs» of the 15th and 16th century, coming from the Low Countries. The most famous specimen is the «Dame à la Licorne», made of six pieces, five of which represent the allegories of the senses.

COLLÈGE DE FRANCE

It was initially called «Collège des trois langues» and was founded by Francis I in 1530, on request of the humanist Guillaume Budé, to make possible a new teaching independent from the Sorbonne.

The first rooms date back to the reign of Henry IV (1594-1610); they were built in the place of the Gaul-Roman «large spa». The buildings were reconstructed by Chalgrin in 1718, modified in the 19th century and enlarged since 1930.

The Roman institution became «Collège de France» during the revolution; famous men taught there, such as the scientists Cuvier, Ampère, Berthelot, the historians Champollion and Michelet, the philosophers Bergson and Gabriel Marcel, the poet Paul Valéry.

THE SORBONNE

It was founded in 1293 by Robert de Sorbon, confessor of Saint Louis, and became rapidly the centre of Christian theology, drawing students from the whole of Europe, from Asia Minor and even from Africa. Among the professors we mention the franciscan Saint Bonaventura and the dominicans Saint Albertus Magnus and Saint Thomas Aquinas.

Its political role was determinative in the conviction of the Templars on the part of Philip the Fair, or of Joan of Arc during the Hundred Years' War. It opposed the Reformation and illuministic philosophy.

The medieval buildings were substituted by a wider Sorbonne, under the impulse of its rector, cardinal Richelieu, who laid the foundation stone in 1627. He devoted himself to the chapel; he entrusted Jacques Lemercier, first architect of the king, with the realization of it. The main façade, of Jesuitic style, faces a square built in

La Sorbonne, founded by the canon Robert de Sorbon in 1293, today seat of the Faculty of Literature.

that epoch, today called «place de la Sorbonne». The side façade, onto the courtyard of honour, has a fine arrangement in steps: staircases, columns supporting a triangular pediment, north transept, dome. The interior of the chapel was deprived, during the revolution, of wood coverings, sculptures, paintings, altars. The medallions with the Fathers of the Church, painted by Philippe de Champaigne on the dome pendentives are left, and above all the funeral monument of cardinal Richelieu, a magnificent tomb in white marble, sculptured by Girardon.

Among the buildings of the classical epoch, only the chapel has remained intact. The university is a work by Nénot between 1885 and 1907, under the Third Republic. Remarkable above all the tower-shaped astronomic observatory.

THE PANTHÉON

View of the Parisian life near the Panthéon.

This lay necropolis, erected on the highest point of the left bank, was conceived as a church. Louis XV decided its construction after a vow made at Metz during his illness. His expression of gratitude towards Providence was united to the project of the canons of Sainte-Geneviève's Abbey, who wished to substitute their ruined chapel. Their abbey had been in fact on the top of the hill since when Clovis had founded it. At the beginning of the 13th century, on the occasion of the opening of rue Clovis, their buildings were destroyed, apart from the 13th-century refectory — now facing rue

Clothilde — and the church bell-tower, called «tour Clovis». These remains are incorporated in the Lyceum Henry IV.

To build the new church of Sainte-Geneviève, Soufflot was appointed. The funds were provided by increasing the prices of lottery tickets but, being that not sufficient, the advancement of work slowed down and, at Soufflot's death in 1780, the work was not complete. That was however the completion of his career as a leader of the «neoclassical» movement, whose ambition was to wed «the lightness of Gothic architecture to the magnificence of Greek ar-

The Panthéon, temple of glory for the great men of the French liberty.

The interior.

chitecture».

Since then the Panthéon has undergone several modifications under the architectural point of view, an expression of the changes in the purpose of the building caused by the succession of the French political regimes.

In 1791 the Constituent Assembly decreed the deconsecration of the church, which would receive the «ashes of the great men of the epoch of French freedom». Napoleon I brought the church back to cult, Louis-Philippe laicized it again, Napoleon III turned it into a «national basilica». The transfer of the ashes of Victor Hugo in 1885 contributed to the decision towards a new laicization. The sentence «the country is grateful to great men» is written on the pediment.

This grand monument is 83 metres high and has a Greek-cross plan. The peristyle, with 22 Corynthian columns, and the garlands sculptured under the trabeation, adorn the façades. The lantern-shaped dome, finished in 1790, is

reinforced with an iron framework. The weight is about 10,000 tons.

Interior: simple but solemn. The laying out of the Corynthian columns and of the pillars of the cross vault, the fine capitals, the domes, the tribunes with balustrades, the arcades, make a harmonious whole. Among the mural paintings, works of the Third Republic, remarkable those telling Sainte-Geneviève's life by Puvis de Chavannes. The dome is decorated with a fresco by Gros ordered by Napoleon in 1811. The crypt with Doric columns, containing the tombs, is divided into several corridors. The revolution buried there Mirabeau and three years later Marat. Then Voltaire and Rousseau were buried there, and then some dignitaries of the First Empire. Under the Third Republic Victor Hugo, Emile Zola, Jean Jaurès and many others were buried here. Gambetta's heart was laid into an urn in 1920. In 1964 a great ceremony took place in honour of Jean Moulin, symbol of the French Resistance.

Perspective from the portico of the Panthéon.

SAINT-ETIENNE-DU-MONT

The history of this church is linked to the one of Sainte-Geneviève's Abbey. At the beginning of the 13th century the abbatial church resulted too small and it was necessary to build a parish church which was placed side by side with it. It was dedicated to Saint-Etienne. At the end of the 15th century this one too resulted too small. It was therefore substituted with the one we know.

The work started from the choir and the bell-tower in 1492, late Gothic period; in the 16th century nave and transept are erected; the foundation stone of the façade is laid by queen Margot, first wife of Henry IV, in 1610, while French Renaissance is blossoming. These differences in style confer originality to the church without affecting its unity. The façade attracts attention in a special way: it is a very successful matching of Gothic and Renaissance elements, accomplished with the superimposition of three pediments. The bell-tower, slightly recessed, accentuates the verticality with its slenderness.

The interior is Gothic, even if some Renais-

Church of Saint-Etienne-du-Mont.

Beside the Panthéon of Jubé.

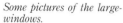

Some pictures of the large-windows.

sance element is present, such as the round small arcades of the aisles. Everything harmonizes: the large luminous glass windows, the powerful balustrade, the flamboyant cross-vault, the ogives of the choir, the round pillars of the nave. The virtuosity is evident in the central kcystone, which forms a fall of 5.50 metres, and in the transversal gallery («jubé») for preaching. It is even peculiarly famous in that it is the last one in Paris, since the other ones were demolished in the 13th century. Its big loop-shaped arch allows the faithful to see the choir, contrary to the other galleries. It is flanked with two staircases twisting around poles and serving the balustrade. Elegant «Renommées» with palms adorn the corner stones. The central part, certainly built according to Philibert Delorme's design, is Renaissance. The side doors, of more classical make, date back to the 17th century.

The glass windows are fine examples of this art in the 16th and 17th century. As for the preacher's pulpit and the organ case, both of the 17th century, they are remarkable for their sculptures.

Sainte-Geneviève's shrine contains some relics, since her sarcophagus was violated during the revolution. It is in gilded copper and dates back to the Second Empire.

Behind the apse, the churchyard: it was surrounded by a cloister one wing of which remains today, adorned with stained-glass windows (beginning of the 17th century) with fine scenes in contrasting colours, such as «le pressoir mystique» or «le vaisseau mystique».

The catechism chapel has been added in the 19th century by Baltard.

Place de la Contrescarpe.

PLACE DE LA CONTRESCARPE

This was built in the last century in the «Mouffe» quarter, full of «cabarets» and confusion. It is still full of animation today.

RUE MOUFFETARD

The silent roads of this point of the Montagne Sainte-Geneviève contrasts with the pictoresque rue Mouffetard, a colourful market which maintains the rustic character of the ancient «bourg Saint-Médard». This continuation of the Paris of

Two pictures of the market in rue Mouffetard.

yesterday (under its provincial appearance) is found above all in the lower part of the road, with its stalls with their merchandise on display.

Rue Mouffetard crosses the «Mouffe» quarter and goes down from place de la Contrescarpe to the **church of Saint-Médard.**

ARÈNE DE LUTÈCE

On the right: church of Saint-Médard.

Arènes de Lutèce.

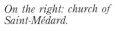

As the Gallic-Roman Lutetia was a small town, it had a building which served as a theatre and as an amphitheatre, that is gladiator games, hunting of wild animals and theatrical spectacles were held there. This monument, undiscovered when the Monge was opened in 1869, only gave a pale image of what it once was.

Only some steps and the stage platform with the adjacent small rooms remain.

THE JARDIN DES PLANTES

In 1626, Louis 13 decided to make the «royal garden» at the request of his doctor, Guy de la Brosse, who was an enthusiastic supporter of the virtues of medicinal plants. More than thousand varieties were cultivated in this garden which rapidly became the experimental branch of the new botanical school. This science was developed under the influence of Fagon who was doctor to Louis XIV. Tournefort, then the Jussiens, enriched the garden, thanks to their travels in Europe and Asia.

On the small mount where the future labyrinth would be built, the first Libanese ceder tree to be planted in France was placed, which, according to legend, had been brought from Syria in 1734 by Bernard de Jussien in his hat, watered every day with his water ration... Buffon is considered the most important gardener of the «Jardin des plantes» due to the enormous amount of work he put into it; he extended the garden until it reached the Seine, completed the collection, created the labyrinth and had the arcades with curious exemplaries constructed. His prestige was such that his statue, in the courtyard of the garden, was inaugurated while he was still alive. The revolution rebaptized the «Royal Garden», «Museum of National History» and «Jardin des Plantes». The hippopotamus, the old lion and the ostrich of the kings at Versailles joined the menagerie created by Geoffroy Saint-Hilaire, other animals were then added, and their arrival was an occasion greatly celebrated by the Parisians, the most famous was perhaps the unloading of the first giraffe at Marseille, in 1828, a gift from the Pasha of Egypt to Charles X. The museum of the 19th century can be remembered by the famous names which are connected to it; Lamark, Lacépède, Cuvier and many other scholars. At the present day the activity of its research and teaching is still being continued.

Going into the garden by the main entrance in rue Cuvier, you will cross the main courtyard of the hôtel de Magnes, a building of the 17th century rebuilt for administrative reasons.

The small communes are of a rustic simplicity, fascinating because they are exceptional to Paris. The house in which Cuvier lived is facing the amphitheatre, a rare Parisien monument built during the revolution. Through winding tree lined avenues you will arrive at the summit of the labirinth, where Verniguet erected one of the most ancient metallic constructions, a Chinese kiosk, according to the tradition of the 18th century. The mystery of this place brings back the romantic atmosphere sought after in the 18th century.

The winter garden, containing 50.000 exotic plants, is a great attraction. In the 19th century the naïf painter Henri Rousseau (called Le Douanier) loved to go there to surround himself with the humid atmosphere of tropical forests. The alpine garden, arranged with streams, rocks and small hills, has a gathering of plants from the Himalayas, Corsica, the Alps...

The zoological zone is populated by wild animals, birds and reptiles. Its creation during the revolution had an educative aim intended to eliminate animal tamers.

Jardin des Plantes.

QUARTIER SAINT-SÉVERIN

Rue Julien le Pauvre.

This quarter has kept part of its medieval fascination, which can be found in the names of the roads and in the embossed work of the façade of the ancient houses.

This is a strange cosmopolitan quarter, a meeting place between culture and tourism, which is perpetually invaded by heterogeneous crowd, formed mostly by foreigners, in the restaurants, cinemas and in the «cantine» where jazz is played.

PLACE SAINT-MICHEL

This is a place much visited by tourists, students and drivers.

The fountain, a work by Davioud, was placed there, under Napoleon III, on the wall of the first building which forms the corner of bd. Saint-Michel with rue Hautefeuille.

This is an important crossroad and an access point for various quarters in the centre of Paris:

The fountain, made by Davioud, which forms the corner between rue Saint-Michel and rue Hautefeuille.

Boulevard Saint-Michel.

in fact it opens to the north towards the Ile de la Cité, to the west towards the Saint-Germain quarter and to the south towards the Quartier Latin through the bd. Saint-Michel.

On the parapet along the Seine are the typical «casse» green bottle of the «bouquinistes» (sellers of used books), which overflow with old posters, post cards, stamps and of course old editions of books. Two side roads cross the Seine parapet: rue Xavier Privas and rue du Chat qui Pêche, they both lead to the Saint-Séverin quarter.

ÉGLISE SAINT-SÉVERIN

Two pictures of the church of Saint-Séverin.

The changes made during the centuries have taken nothing away from the fascination and harmony of this church, considered to be one of the masterpieces of late gothic art.

It is named for a hermit of the 6th century who, according to legend, miraculously cured king Clovis.

Work on the present church was started in the 13th century. The first three trellises and the lower floors of the bell-tower remain.

In the 15th century the church was enlarged with other trellises, the southern side nave, the double northern side nave, the apse, the cloisters and the higher part of the bell-tower with the spire.

The last works in the side chapels, covered

by pinioned roofs, were finished towards 1530. The elliptic chapel, which is more recent, goes back to XVII. The door is from the church of Saint-Pierre-Boeuf, demolished in the Île de la Cité.

The interior was transformed according to the wishes of the «Grande Mademoiselle», sister of Louis XIV. The choir was arranged by Lebrun; its pillars and archways were faced in marble and painted wood.

The axial spiral pillar, from which a multitude of ribbing is born, creates a strange play of light and shade and is a perfect example of the mastery of gothic art.

The magnificent organ case of the 18th century has contributed to make Saint-Severin a place of concerts of both classical and organistic music.

Saint Julien le Pauvre.

ÉGLISE SAINT-JULIEN-LE-PAUVRE

This small humble church, with a rustic appearance, is well matched with the old houses with their irregular façades which surround it. It was built in the 6th century in a strategic point on the left bank. where the two main Roman roads cross.

Initially it was the chapel of a hostel for travellers with no means; it was then destroyed at the time of the Norman invasion in 886.

In the 12th century it was handed over to the Longpont Benedectine abbey which built a priory on its foundations. Built between 1175 and 1220, it is of the same period as the Notre-Dame and brings to memory many other churches of the Middle Ages which were built around the latter.

It was seat of university assemblies until 1524, a year in which some students laid it to waste; following this episode they were forbidden to use it again.

During the revolution it was closed and transformed into a salt warehouse and then into a wool exhibition. Lastly it was used as a warehouse until 1826, when it became the Chapelle of the Hôtel Dieu.

On the 28th March 1889 it was officiated in the melchite rite.

From an architectonical point of view in this church, the passage from the Romanesque style, which has given it solidity and simplicity, to the gothic style can be seen.

The shortening of the church has brought to light an old well of the 12th century, with the well curb in stone and an iron grating.

In the 17th century, the façade, the right side naves and the doorway were rebuilt, while the naves on the left were transformed into a sacristy.

Inside the church the numerous capitals of the choir, the nave and the apsedes, sculptured with acanthus leaves, is noteworthy.

Flanking the church, the ancient closed garden which has become Viviani square, protects one of the oldest trees in Paris. The tree is a locust robinia tree, helped up by a prop, and was planted in 1601 by Robin, who gave it his name.

This is a pretty and restful place, in a tumultuous quarter, and offers a unique view of the Notre-Dame and the Île de la Cité.

Church of Saint Julien le Pauvre.

Fountain «Wallace».

MONTPARNASSE

Between the 6th, 14th and 15th arrondissement is the Montparnasse quarter, its centre is formed by the carrefour of the Montparnasse and Raspail boulevards.

It is delimited to the north by rue d'Assas and rue de Vaugirard, to the south by boulevard Pasteur and to the east by avenue du Général Leclerc and avenue Denfert Rochereau.

THE MONTPARNASSE OF YESTERDAY. In the 17th century, Queen Margot (first wife of Henry IV) expelled the students from Pré aux Clercs. They emigrated to the south of Paris onto a hill created by the embankments from the surrounding quarries. They called this hill Mont Parnasse, referring to the place in which, according to the ancient Greeks, Apollo and the Muses lived.

The present Montparnasse was countryside until the 18th century; in the 6th and 7th

Tour Montparnasse.

centuries the abbey of Saint-Germain-des-Prés came into the possession of Val Girard (from the abbot Girard de Moret) who gave his name to the boulevard and rue de Vaugirard.

The village of Vaugirard subsequently arose, surrounded by the property of rich Parisian families.

At the end of the 18th century M.me Suzanne Necker created a hospice in the ex Benedectine monastery of Notre-Dame-de-Liesse (it was later called the Necker hospital in her honour).

In this building she inaugurated a complex system of aeration, based on a theory which was very diffused at that time, according to which air evacuates pathogenic microbes. In spite of this the number of deaths there was much higher than in other Parisian hospitals.

Beside this building is the «Hospice de l'Enfant Jésus», which supplied the entire quarter with milk and butter thanks to its herd of 100 cows.

In 1761 the hill was demolished, in order to realize the present boulevard Montparnasse (which was then a fragment of the Fermiers Généraux town wall). The top of the hill was then to be found in the present carrefour Vauvin.

After the revolution and until the end of the 19th century, Montparnasse was a place of amusement, much frequented by people who loved parties.

They used to meet in the «guinguettes» and in the fashion-able cabarets, such as the «Elysée Matignon», the «Grande Chaumière» or the «Bal de l'Arc-en-ciel».

In 1860, Haussmann opened boulevard de l'Enfer, boulevard d'Arago and rue de Rennes, thus connecting the quarter to Paris.

THE BOHÈME OF MONTPARNASSE.
At the beginning of the 20th century, together with the École de Paris, Montparnasse had its greatest artistic effervescence.

Many foreign artists (Brancusi, Modigliani, Chagall, Soutine, Foujita...), who had come to Paris to find the necessary conditions for their artistic maturity, met in the literary cafés of the Boulevard.

Every Tuesday evening the numerous disciples of Paul Fort, the «Prince of Poets» met at «La Closerie des Lilas».

Behind the «Closerie des Lilas», at the carrefour of the Observatoire — where Marshal Ney was killed — there is his beautiful statue by Rude.

The Carrefour Vauvin and the 4 famous «Brasseries» which can be found there («Le Dôme», «Le Select», «La Coupole», and «La Ro-

Restaurant Dôme.

On the left: the quarters of Montparnasse and the Brasserie La Coupole.

A café at Montparnasse.

tonde») have been the cultural centre of the quarter for a long time. Poets (Cendrars, A. Breton, J. Cocteau), political exiles (Trotzky, Lenin), musicians (Satie, Stravinsky) and other not less famous artists such as Picasso, Hemingway or Eisenstein used to meet there.

At this same crossroads is the statue of Balzac by Rodin. This superb work of art which stirred up considerable controversy at the time of its erection in 1939, is a magnificent example of the immense talent of its author.

MONTPARNASSE OF TODAY. After the IInd world war, Montparnasse has changed face. It is still very fashionable with its many cafés, cabarets and night clubs frequented by artists and lovers of amusement and is still one of the most lively places in Paris.

However, in spite of the fact that some artists and writers still live there, Montparnasse is no longer the quarter it was at the beginning of the century. The vast urbanistic project carried out in 1960 has contributed to change the aspect of this quarter which, from very popular, has become a great and lively business centre.

THE MAINE-MONTPARNASSE OPERATION. This was born from a project elaborated in 1934 by Paul Dautry who proposed to create an important business centre comparable with that of the Défense to the south of Paris.

This operation started with the demolition of the ex station of Montparnasse which freed a space of 14 hectares. In fact it was here that, on the 24th August 1944, General von Choltitz signed the act of surrender of his garrison.

The new station, with a U shape, was built to the south of this area. The Tour Montparnasse, at the time of its construction, gave rise to considerable controversy which revived interest in the quarter. It is 209 m high, shaped like a truncated almond and does not lack in class.

From the 58th floor there is a magnificent

Théâtre de la Gaieté: detail.

view of a «full sized relief map of Paris». The perspective of Montparnasse, Tour Eiffel and the Défense is wonderful.

To the south of this complex, in a stupefying vertical unity, the modern buildings of Montparnasse rise upwards, such as the white «Montparnasse Park Hôtel», the «Building Vaugirard» or the «Super Montparnasse», with the façade relief in prefabricated cement.

To the south west, on boulevard Vaugirard, is the Musée de la Poste (the Postal Museum), with the blind façade decorated with polytrigonal sculptures.

Not far from here is the Musée Bourdelle, its model is the artist's house; here the most beautiful works of the famous sculptor are gathered.

In 1982 the architect Riccardo Boffils was entrusted with the project for a space situated to the south of the present station. The result is a calm, peaceful and fresh place. Its composition, in a style inspired by neo-classicism, unites a futuristic conception (mastodontical columns in metalized glass) to the harmonious proportions of the Greek-Roman buildings.

THE CIMETIÈRE DU SUD. Called «du Montparnasse», it is certainly one of the richest in sepulchres of famous people (Baudelaire, Saint-Saëns, Sarre, Rude, Soutine...) and in sculptures («Le Baiser» by Brancusi).

RUE DE LA GAITÉ. This famous road, which ows its name (good humour) to the many restaurants, cabarets and places of amusement which have always flanked it, is trying to keep up its fame; at present sex-shops are ever more numerous.

There are still four theatres there: the «Théâtre Montparnasse», with its façade decorated with polychrome stuccoes (at the end of the XIXth century Paul Fort had his vanguard plays performed there); the «Théâtre de la Gaité Montparnasse», the «Grand Edgar» and a tiny theatre, typical of the Paris of yesterday, «La Comédie Italienne». There are still some façades — testimony to the life here during the «mad years» — such as the very characteristic wooden one of the «Week-end Club», which represents a windmill with its sails painted in red.

LA RUCHE. After being threatened with demolition, the Ruche, ex wine pavilion in the Exhibition in 1900, elaborated by Eiffel and rebuilt in 1902 in the passage Dantzig, is part of the history of art in the 20th century. Succeeding the Bâteau-Lavoir, it was a lodging and study for Chagall, Soutine, Zadkine and Léger, and for Cendrars and Cuny to day-dream.

In this way, keeping one of the last artist centres of Montparnasse alive, we conserve a testimony of the effervescent artistic past of this quarter.

TROCADÉRO - ÉCOLE MILITAIRE

The O.R.T.F. Building (French Radio and Television Centre)

*It is impossible to separate the monuments which make up the perspective of the Trocadéro. The **Military School** with the **Champ de Mars** obliged Monsieur Eiffel and his tower and then the architects assigned to the construction of Palais de Chaillot for International Exhibitions, to carry out their work within this magnificent perspective.*

*The tourist attraction formed by the **Eiffel tower**, the **Palais de Chaillot** and the Champ de Mars is also an ideal space due to its enormity, for demonstrations of every kind: fireworks, the starting point of races, open air concerts... At the feet of the «Grande Dame» (the Eiffel tower), the 24 hour motor boat race takes place on the Seine.*

PALAIS DE CHAILLOT

The hill of Chaillot was chosen by Napoleon I in order to build an enormous palace for his son, King of Rome. This idea however, remained nothing more than a plan due to the fall of the Empire, even if the hill was leveled and the Jéna bridge built.

This hill was used by Charles X in 1827 to prepare the seizure of Cadice and of the Trocadéro fortress in Spain.

The International Exhibition in 1878 was the occasion in which the Palais du Trocadéro was built. The palace was substituted in 1937 by the Palais de Chaillot built by Carlu, Azéma and Boileau for the International Exhibition of that year.

It is formed by two monumental pavilions with curved semicircular wings, separated by a wide terrace with a view in perspective of the Military School; bronze gilded statues adorn the sides.

On the façade of the Palace are inscriptions in golden letters dictated by the poet Paul Valéry and this building is the seat of various museums:

Panoramic view of the Seine, the gardens of Trocadéro and Palais Chaillot.

Palais Chaillot and Trocadéro.

— the «*Musée des Monuments Français*» (Museum of French Monuments), in the wing towards Paris, illustrates the evolution of architecture and art.

— the «*Musée de la Marine*» (the Marine Museum), in the wing towards Passy, which flanks the *Musée de l'Homme* (the Museum of Man), concerning the different races of mankind.

Under the terrace, the famous **Théâtre National Populaire** (NPT, the National Popular Theatre) — with a large hall for performances which is much appreciated for the acoustics there — is considered a famous place for dramatic art.

At the beginning Jean Vilar with an excellent company, among whom were Maria Casarès and Gérard Philippe, attracted a considerable audience.

The gardens are reached by stairs decorated with bass-reliefs and sculptures, work of 40 artists. At the centre, with perfect respect for the alignment of the terrace, is an immense basin bordered by golden stone and bronze sculptures, which offer a marvelous play of water, especially at night when the lighting creates a magical atmosphere.

The gardens, shaded on every side, slope gently down to the banks of the Seine.

View of the Seine near the Eiffel Tower.

The Eiffel Tower.

The Eiffel Tower: bust of Eiffel.

TOUR EIFFEL

This tower is, in a certain sense, the emblem of Paris.

Its dimensions and conception are surprising and unique and it represents the synthesis of engineering and architecture.

Illuminated from the ground upwards, at night it shines dominating the other monuments; by day it gives an incomparable view of the whole of Paris.

The Eiffel Tower: effective view.

The Eiffel Tower. Detail of the first floor.

It represents the ingenuity, creativity and conquest of mankind.

It was created for the International Exhibition in 1889. This was the age of the industrial revolution. At this time it was necessary to use new materials in order to enter the new modern age. In 1885 various projects for a tower of 300 m height were compared and the project by G. Eiffel was taken into consideration.

The final decision raised numerous protests. The newspaper «Le Temps» published the petition of the «300», in which, among others were the names of Gounot, Maupassant, Dumas the younger... They denounced the dishonour of Paris: «Will the image of Paris be for ever more associated with the bizarre, mercantile ideas of a construction of machines, in order to be rendered ugly and dishonoured? For 20 years shall we have to see the widening as of an ink stain, the hateful shadow of a column of bolted steel».

In spite of these criticisms the erecting yard was opened on the 26th January 1887 and the enormous work project was started. At the end of 1887 only the first floor had been built. It was not until 1889 that the last nail was sent home; on this occasion there was a small cerimony among workers and engineers, during which G. Eiffel pronounced a famous phrase: «The tricolour flag will be the only one in the world to fly on top of a pole 300 metres high».

Its role in the field of communications has allowed it to stand up to various «attacks». In fact, during the 1st World War it became the transmitting radio station. In 1916 it made the first transatlantic wireless communications possible. The first transmissions of the TSF (Wireless telegraph) created by Gen. Férié (1921) were also sent from its summit. Lastly, in 1957 it was provided with an aerial television which brought

The Eiffel Tower seen from Pont Alexandre III.

The Eiffel Tower: nocturnal pictures.

The garden below the Eiffel Tower.

its height to 320,75 m and with two laboratories, one of meterology and the other of air navigation.

This immense tower 320,75 m high, is constructed of 15000 pieces and with intertwined metal beams of extreme lightness. Its feet rest on enormous cement pillars which are capable of bearing the weight of 7000 tons.

The Eiffel tower has three floors: the first is 57 m high, the second 115 and the third 274. For those who wish to ascend, there are elevators which make it possible not to have to climb 1652 steps.

ÉCOLE MILITAIRE

Panorama of a part of the city: an imposing perspective of the Field of Mars and the Military School.

This school still maintains today its military vocation, it is the seat of important schools: École d'Etat Majeur (The Major State School), École Supérieure de Guerre (the Advanced School of War), École Supérieure d'Intendance (The Advanced Superintendence School) and the École des Hautes Études de Défense Nationale (School for further studies on National Defence).

The Military School was created by Louis XV following the suggestion of M.me Pompadour de Pâris Duverney, in order to enable young nobles of impoverished families to follow a military career.

The architect Jacques-Ange Gabriel built the «École Royale Militaire» (The Royal Military School) between 1751 and 1773. In 1776 it had to close due to economical reasons; the pupils were distributed among various provincial colleges, which took their name from the École Militaire.

In 1777 the school was restored as «École Supérieure des Cadets» (the Advanced Cadets' School). Napoleon Bonaparte was a student there in 1784 when he was fifteen years old. He left the school with the degree of second artillery lieutenant.

During the revolution the school was closed, but afterwards it rapidly regained its original functions. The Imperial Guard, the Consular Guard and the Royal Guard (under the Restoration period) alternated there.

The majestic appearance of this group of buildings is rather surprising for a barracks. It's style shows a strong, animated classicism whose lines form a harmonious whole. The central, two-storeyed pavilion which may be seen from the Champ de Mars, is ornamented by eight columns as tall as the building itself.

The importance of the podiment, sculptured with trophics and allegories and crowned by a quadrangular dome, is enhanced by two lower side-wings.

The two barracks on either side are recent: they dats back to the 19th century. On the back, after the sportsground, is the beautiful ceremony courtyard enclosed by two arcades of simple couplod columns in borio order.

In the background is the façade, consisting of three pavilions connected to one another by two wings of columne.

Panoramic view.

LES INVALIDES

Les Invalides: detail.

At the request of Louis XIV, the Hôtel des Invalides by Libéral Bruant was built to the west of faubourg Saint-Germain, on the Grenelle plain which was then still agricultural.

This glamorous building was constructed to shelter mutilated ex soldiers free of charge. Previously the disabled soldiers were sheltered by monasteries (as lay-brothers) or had to beg. The new hotel started to take in its pensioners in 1674; in 1691 there were 5000 of them. Jules Hardouin-Mansart built the first church on the axis of the main courtyard. A few years later he completed this superb monumental complex with a masterpiece: the Église du Dôme. Still today, about 200 disabled soldiers contribute to the continuation of the vocation of the hotel. However the building are mostly occupied by the rich collections of the Musée de l'Armée (The Military Museum). The reign of Louis-Philippe dedicated the Église du Dôme to the memory of Napoleon I preparing his last dwelling there.

Even when he was living at Versailles, Louis XIV was very interested in urban and architectonical works in Paris. Colbert's motto was «Glory and Magnificence» for all the Parisian buildings of the reign. The Académie de l'Architecture (the Academy of Architecture), founded by Louis XIV, created a design imprinted with rigour, symmetry and measure: «classicism». The enormous complex of the Invalides is fruit of this concept: regal order, grandiose character, the hôtel and Dôme are creations of pure classical French art.

The hospital, Libéral Bruant's work, king's architect, was built between 1671 and 1676. It consists of a complex of buildings organized around square avenues. The façade, of an interminable lenght, stretches for about 200 m and is interrupted in the centre by an imposing curvilinear doorway. The frontage is surmounted by an equestrian relief of Louis XIV, dressed in Roman clothes, between Justice and Prudence. These statues were carried out in 1815 by Cartlier and are copies of the original works by Coustou (1735). On both sides of the doorway there is no decoration apart from the military motifs which cover the garrets, and the two side pavilions. The Honour courtyard is surrounded on all four sides by structures with two floors of arcades with two orders of arches. The austerity of the buildings is slightly lessened by a few moderate decorations: the four overhanging pavilions with their decorated façades like a frieze, the bull's eye groups decorated with trophies and in the corners, four sculptured groups representing the impetuosity of warhorses crushing the symbols of war. The large dimensions of this courtyard make it suitable for military parades.

The pavilion at the end of the courtyard of Honour, forms the façade of the church which J.H. Mansart projected for the hôtel (1679-1708). It was called «église des soldats» (soldiers' church) or «église Saint-Louis-des-Invalides». The central luminous nave is framed by side naves surmounted by galleries. At the top of these are standards and flags taken from the enemy during the campaigns of the 19th and 20th centuries. Some funerary monuments are leaning against pillars.

In the page beside: Les Invalides, interior of the church and tomb of Napoleon.

View with the church of Saint-Louis in the foreground.

Les Invalides: church of Saint Louis.

The Dôme des Invalides was built between 1679 and 1706 by J.H.-Mansart. Here the king's architect has shown an exceptional geniality. He was not only able to adapt (and turn to account) the new church with the complex — it seems that the severe horizontal line of the façade of the hotel has been stretched out in order to enhance the dome — but above all he has made this church into an apogee of classicism. A result of the architectonical shapes experimented at Carmes and Val de Grâce, the Dôme inherits the superimposition of the orders crowned by a dome from the «Jesuitical» churches. However the absence of wings, the vertical energy of the lengthening of the dome, the neatness of volumes in the opposition between cube and cilinder, are Mansart's innovations which herald the art of the 18th century (the rococo and neoclassical styles).

The cubic footing is composed of superimposed gothic and corinthian orders, surmounted by a triangular frontage. The double tambour of the dome, in the foreground is marked by windows from the Corinthian buttresses and the attic is decorated with a balustrade and dormer windows. The slender proportions of the dome and its 12 ribbings, the presence of the skylights and the spire, complete the powerful upward harmony of the building. This dôme is the highest in Paris and perhaps the most elegant.

The interior. The adoption of a central plan, fashionable at the time, inserts the Greek cross into a square. Until the revolution, an altar which the two churches had in common, was surmounted by a canopy, an influence of Saint-Peter's in Rome. The sculpture was directed by Girardon and the painting of the dome is by Charles de la Fosse. In the 19th century the church was changed: it was separated from the soldiers' church by a large glass pannel placed there by Crépinet in 1873 and, above all, it became the burial place of Napoleon I. The return (from Saint-Elena) of the ashes of the emperor was organized during the reign of Louis-Philippe, in 1840, but the funerary architectonical project was finished by Visconti under Napoleon III in 1861. A circular open cript was dug under the dome. In the centre is the sarcophagus in red porphyry from Finland on a green granite base from the Vosges. The emperor rests there dressed in the uniform of colonel of the Vieille Garde mounted hunters. The complex, in neo-Greek style, is surrounded by 12 enormous statues by Pradier which represent the victorious imperial campaigns.

THE ESPLANADE AND THE AVENUE DE BRETEUIL. A vaste esplanade was prepared in front of the hôtel at the beginning of the 18th century by Robert de Cotte, obtaining a good perspective in this way.

As far as the Eglise du Dôme is concerned, it was shown to the full by the opening of avenue de Breteuil. A previous project endowed the church with a colonnade inspired by that of Bernini at Saint-Peter's in Rome.

Les Invalides and Pont Alexandre III.

Les Invalides.

Les Invalides and Pont Alexandre III.

FROM PLACE DE LA CONCORDE TO THE DÉFENSE

Rather than a quarter, the area which connects Place de la Concorde to the Défense quarter is an immense perspective. The gigantic project concerning this rectilineal has slowly taken shape during the course of the centuries: Place de la Concorde, Champs-Elysées, Arc de Triomphe and lastly the Défense. Its arch, which is still being built, will close this historical parade.

La Marseillaise, one of the eight statues crowning with Place de la Concorde.

PLACE DE LA CONCORDE

This regal square, unique for its dimensions, gives us a double perspective: from east to west it is crossed by a perspective called Voie Triomphale, and from north to south it is cut by a smaller perspective limited by the Madeleine and by the Palais Bourbon.

The square was created at the request of the municipal magistrates of Paris, who wanted to erect the statue of Louis XV. The architect Jacques-Ange Gabriel planned it with an hexagonal shape, with 8 pavilions at the corners and surrounded by dry ditches, protected by balustrades. The equestrian statue is by Bouchardon.

Each regime gave it a new name: Place Louis XV became Place de la Révolution, where the guillotines were to be found, including that which beheaded Louis XVI on 21st January 1793.

At the end of the 17th century, under the Directory, full of hope and peace, it took the name of Place de la Concorde.

It was only under Louis-Philippe that it assumed its final appearance. Ingeniously he decided to decorate the centre, not with some symbolical monuments which would perhaps be short-lived, but with an obelisk built 33 centuries before, from the temple of Luxor, which had been given to Charles X by the Egyptian viceroy Mehemet Ali.

This was how this monolith in pink granite covered with hieroglyphs, weighing 220 t, was erected on its pedestal in 1836.

The architect Hittorff planned two fountains, inspired by those in Saint-Peter's square in Rome: they are formed by two basins with symbolical figures (rivers, oceans, fishing, navigation, harvest). The square is completed by statues of women who represent the largest towns in France and they are situated above the 8 pavilions.

Two pairs of horses frame the entrances to the park: the winged horses by Coysevox, sculptured with extreme lightness of style, which represent Fame and Mercury; these can be found at the entrance of the Tuileries and come from the Marly Castle trough.

The Champs-Elysées entrance to the park is adorned with the beautiful «Marly» horses sculptured by Coustou.

Place de la Concorde.

La Madeleine seen from Place de la Concorde.

Effective and particular pictures of the fountains in Place de la Concorde.

CHAMPS-ELYSÉES

This immense avenue is dominated by the imposing Arc de Triomphe which is famous all over the world.

The Champs-Elysées, enlivened by a cosmopolitan crowd in search of amusement, are also the seat of important military parades on the 14th July and 11th November, when they are adorned with flags and lights of the same colours. At Christmas they have a very different appearance: garlands of light make them shine and sparkle.

AVENUE DES CHAMPS-ELYSÉES

This elegant avenue was an initiative of Maria de Medici who had this long walk, lined with elms, along the Seine, built, from the Tuileries until the present Place de l'Alma: it was called Cours de la Reine.

With the aim of lengthening the perspective of the Tuileries, Le Nôtre were the first to open the Grand Cours here in 1667, which later took the name of Champs-Elysées,

In 1724 the Duke d'Antin enlarged and lengthened the avenue until it reached the Butte Chaillot (the present Place de l'Etoile); his work

was continued until the Neuilly bridge by his successor, the Marquis of Marigny.

In 1774 Soufflot levelled the hill lowering it by 5 m.

The gardens, which were still in a wild state at the end of the 18th century, had a few open air entertainments and dances to offer to the public; however by night this wide avenue was not a very safe place to frequent.

In 1815 the Cossacks set up their camp there and ruined the gardens; it took quite a few years to reorganize them.

In 1828 pavements, fountains and gas lighting were installed there, and under the Second Empire they became the English style gardens of the present day, with their beautiful avenues lined by horse-chestnuts and their pavilions hidden in the greenery and the splendid flowerbeds.

There you can also find the Ledoyen restaurant, which already existed as a simple hotel, under Louis XVI. The «espace Pierre Cardin», the high fashion house, is in the building of the ex Ambassadeurs theatre.

The Marigny theatre, famous in the 19th century, was substituted in 1883 by a panoramic hall containing a series of representations of Paris through the ages, it did not last for very long and the hall became a theatre again. On certain days a week a philatelist market is held beside the theatre.

In the 19th century these places became very fashionable and the aristocracy had magnificent private hotels built, of which, unfortunately, only a few ruins remain. Only the

The Champs Elysées at the end of the Arc de Triomphe.

Entrance portal of the Petit Palais.

«Rond Point des Champs-Elysées» conserves a few buildings of this period. Today you can still see the Palais de Glace, which has become the Théâtre du Rond Point Renaud Barrault, or the façade of the previous seat of the newspaper «Le Figaro».

Thcsc ancient buildings are enhanced by magnificent flowerbeds enlivened by spouts of water into the pools.

After the 1914-'18 war, the private hotels started to disappear to make way for de luxe shops, offices, restaurants and cinemas.

Today the Champs-Elysées, «the most beautiful avenue in the word» has completely lost its private hotels and also its aristocratic exclusiveness.

An enormous crowd wends its way along the wide pavements flanked by shops, cinemas, caffés or famous restaurants such as «Fouquet's», side by side with fast food. There are also the seats of important companies and motor showrooms to be found there.

THE PETIT AND THE GRAND PALAIS

In the gardens of the Champs-Elysées, the Winston Churchill avenue is flanked by the Petit and the Grand Palais. These buildings, constructed for the Universal Exhibition in 1900, are of the style of the period which made use of stone and steel covered with glass.

The Petit Palais has a monumental arcade with a frontage decorated with an allegory which represents the city of Paris among the Muses and it is crowned by a dome. This building contains the Musée des Beaux Arts. There you can admire the Dutuit and Tuck collections

The Grand Palais.

The Petit Palais.

and also masterpieces of French art in the XIXth century.

The more important Grand Palais has an ionic colonnade and walls ornated with mosaic friezes on its façade. The exterior decoration is noteworthy, with the quadrigae of the corner flight of steps and the modern style figures.

Inside the building, a splendid staircase winds under an immense window at 43 m from the ground, crowned by a shallow dome. Various exhibitions were held here many years ago. At present it holds temporary exhibitions of great value. A part of the building is dedicated to a museum of scientific popularization: the Palais de la Découverte, created at the time of the Exposition Internationale des Arts et Techniques (International Exhibition of Arts and Techniques) in 1937.

ARC DE TRIOMPHE

The Arc de Triomphe.

Place Charles de Gaulle, still often called Place de l'Étoile due to the large avenues around it, underlines the avenue des Champs Elysées with the monumental Arc de Triomphe.

Which position could have been better for Napoleon, to erect a triumphal arch dedicated to the glory of his Grande Armée? So Napoleon I, from various projects of every kind (pyramids, a statue of liberty or even a gigantic elephant), chose the more classical project by Jean Chal-

Panoramic view of the Arc de Triomphe.

Details of the Arc de Triomphe: «the triumph of 1810» (by Cortot) represents the peace treaty in Wien; «la Marseillaise» (by Rude) commemorates the departure of the volunteers in 1792.

In the following page a nocturnal view of the Arc de Triomphe with light effects.

Arc de Triomphe at night.

new avenues which Haussmann added to the 4 which already existed. In addition, the 12 hotels planned by Hittorff contribute to the geometry of the square.

The Arc de Triomphe is formed by a large central arch and by a smaller side one, which make it perfectly proportioned. The sculptures which decorate it are the work of Thiers. To the east, the right side was sculptured by Rude: «le Départ des Volontaires de 1792» (the departure of the Volunteers of 1792), more widely known as «la Marseillaise» (the Marseillaise), a real masterpiece full of energy and impetus.

The other side, sculptured by Cortot, represents «Le Triomphe de Napoléon» (Napoleon's Triumph), the west side was decorated by Etex with conventional groups; «La Paix» (Peace) and «La Résistance» (Resistance).

Above these groups, the tympanums are occupied with representations of Fame by Pradier; at the same height there are scenes representing important events during the Empire: Marceau's funeral, the battles of Aboukir, Alexandria, Arcole, Austerlitz and Jemappes.

Under the trabeation, a frieze 137 m long circles the façade. Six sculptors, paid by the metre, managed to represent «giants» with a height of 2.12 m, in memory of the departure and return of the armies.

Since the 1914-18 war there is a stone under the Arc de Triomphe which covers the tomb of the Unknown Warrior, a flame which is lighted every evening keeps vigil over it.

At the top of the Arch, visitors can admire an exceptional panorama of the perspective from the Louvre to the Défense and of the «Étoile» (star) formed by 12 avenues.

Avenue Foch, which reaches the Bois de Boulogne, has kept its dignified style and is the widest avenue measuring 120 m across, flanked by tall trees.

grin. Work started in 1806 on the hill of Chaillot, chosen for its immense perspective.

In 1810, for the ceremony of the entrance of Maria Luisa into the capital, a life sized canvas simulacrum painted «trompe-l'oeil» style was displayed.

A year later Chalgrin died and the construction of the Arc de Triomphe was given to one of his pupils: Goust.

With the arrival of the Allies work was interrupted and was only taken up again under Louis XVIII. The inauguration did not take place until the 29th July 1836.

The Arc de Triomphe has kept the appearance which we know today. The arch 50 m high was enhanced by the spreading of the 8

La Défense: view.

THE DÉFENSE

This is a modern quarter which is aligned with the lengthening of the Tuileries-Arc de Triomphe perspective and for which a conclusion has recently been found.

This business quarter has settled on the Butte de Chantecoq, and on its summit is a cross roads made in 1765 on the axis of avenue de Neuilly. The name Défense was given to it in 1871 after the siege of Paris.

In the 18th century this cross roads should have been integrated into the gigantic project for the opening of the triumphal road which leads to the Étoile de Noailles, in the forest of Saint-Germain-en-Laye.

However an urbanistic project for this quarter was not studied until 1955. Its aim was to renew the road network, to reduce the concentration of offices in the capital and to create flats.

The first new building was that of the C.N.I.T. (Centre National des Industries et des Techniques - National Centre of Industry and

La Défense: Tour Manhattan.

Technique) which was inaugurated in 1957 and destined for exhibitions and halls. This large palace with the unusual shape of a shell, is at the top of the ex hill.

The management of this great initiative was given to E.P.A.D. (Etablissement Public pour l'Aménagement de la Défense - Istitute for the Arrangement of the Défence) who decided to pave the central axis with an enormous stone reserved for pedestrians, which would cover the R.E.R. (in 1969) and the S.N.C.F. road networks and also many car parks.

The initial project has been greatly enlarged and now the Défense has become a universe of steel, cement and glass. However the towers mark the central perspective which widens into a green space, dotted with sculptures and vegetation.

To the west the esplanade is occupied, on one side by a large commercial centre, «Les quatre temps», and on the other by C.N.I.T. Magnificent plays of water spout into a large basin to the rhythm of music.

Towards the Seine, to the east is the Tête de la Défense — the conclusion, finally decided, of the famous perspective — consists of a gigantic hollow cube, projected by the Danish architect, Johan Otto Von Spreckelsen. This immense arch, with a height and width of 105 m, unites power, elegance and simplicity. The roof of the arch will certainly offer a fantastic view. Construction work, started in 1985, should be finished in 1988.

La Défense: Tour Neptune.

La Défense.

Palais de l'Elysée: the guards.

QUARTER OF FAUBOURG SAINT-HONORÉ

*Rue du Faubourg Saint-Honoré stretches from place de Beauvau to the Madeleine, it is a focus of Parisian elegance. This road, the ex Chemin du Roulé, has become a place to wander and admire the luxurious shop windows which are magical with their grace and refinement. It is a concentration of the Parisian «chic»; here are antiquarians, perfumers, tailors... whose names are now linked with rue du Faubourg Saint-Honoré in the same way as Hermès, Cardin, Lapidus, Lancôme...; the famous Maxim's restaurant, with its red canopy with golden lettering and its waiters in livery, has also found its place in this luxurious Parisian quarter. The slightly more austere **Palais de l'Elysée** and the **Madeleine** also skirt rue du **Faubourg Saint-Honoré**.*

PALAIS DE L'ELYSÉE

This vast residence with a garden has been the dwelling of the President of the Republic since 1873. It has seen the succession of the 13 presidents of the IIIrd Republic, those of the IInd and those of the Vth.

The palace was built in 1718 by Mollet for the Count of Evreux. In 1753 it was bought by the Marchioness of Pompadour who then bequeathed it to the king; he sold it to the financer Beaujon who had it enlarged.

During the revolution it became national property and was transformed into a public dance hall. Caroline Murat, sister of Napoleon I, lived there for some years and had it restored. Subsequently the Empress Joséphine lived there. After Waterloo, on the 22nd June 1815, Napoleon had to sign his second abdication there.

After his election in 1849, Prince Louis Napoléon Bonaparte settled there and there he prepared the coup d'état of the 2nd December 1851.

Rue St. Honoré, Palais de l'Elysée.

THE MADELEINE

Fauchon shop-window.

The heavy façade of the Madeleine church towers over a footing behind an immense flight of 28 steps with an ancient colonnade, 20 m high, which is connected beyond the Concorde and the Seine, to the twin colonnade of Palais Bourbon. The research for symmetry with the Chambre des Députés brought about the decision to substitute the ex church of Sainte-Madeleine-de-la-Ville-de-l'Evêque with another larger one. Therefore the first stone of the building started by Contant d'Ivry was laid in 1763 by Louis XV.

Work on the building was stopped by the revolution. In 1806 Napoleon gave Vignon the task of erecting a temple to the glory of the soldiers of the Grande Armée. With the fall of the Empire the idea of building a temple was abandoned and Louis XVIII destined the building to be a church, without however changing the project. Finally the church was opened in 1842.

The church of Sainte-Madeleine has remained an enormous ancient temple 108 m long and 43 m wide, surrounded by a colonnade of 52 fluted columns. Under the colonnade 34 niches have

La Madeleine.

La Madeleine: façade.

Maxim's in rue Royal.

Place de la Concorde and Palais Bourbon seen from rue Royal.

been made for statues of saints. The immense façade is decorated with a sculpture by Lemaire which represents the Last Judgement.

The interior consists of only one nave with a semicircular choir. The bass-reliefs in the flat domes represent the apostles, sculptured by Rude, Foyatier and Pradier. The union of the marble coloured with gold gives a general impression of richness.

QUARTIER DE L'OPÉRA

PLACE VENDÔME

Place Vendôme: detail, decorated with three-coloured cockades.

Place Vendôme is today seat of the Parisian de luxe commerce, the privileged position of the most famous jewellers, international banks... and where the well known Hôtel Ritz is also to be found.

This royal square was created between 1687 and 1720 by Jules Hardouin-Mansart in the place of the Hôtel de Vendôme and its gardens, in order to erect an equestrian statue of Louis XIV there, it is one of the most beautiful in the capital for simplicity and austerity. It is octagonal and is surrounded by buildings which open into wide arcades to increase the area and skilfully enlivened by foreparts with a triangular façade supported by built-in columns.

Two unlevel floors are connected by Corinthian pillars and are covered by numerous garrets. At the centre of the square is the column erected by Gondoin and Lepère between 1806 and 1810. Constructed on the model of the Trajan column in Rome, Napoleon dedicated it to his victorious armies. 1200 pieces of artillery captured from the Austrians and Russians were melted to cover it. The shaft of the column is decorated with a spiral series of bass-reliefs in bronze where military engagements are represented for 260 m. The imperial statue at the summit, work of Antoine Denis Chaudet, only remained there for 4 years, and was replaced with every change of regime. Under the revolution it was pulled down and replaced with a statue of Henry IV which, in 1863, made way for a statue of the Emperor. This was demolished by the Commune and was changed permanently 3 years later.

Place Vendôme.

L'OPÉRA

Theatre of the Opéra: sculpture (detail).

Haussmann decided to make the Place de l'Opéra a cosmopolitan meeting place. It is the point where the Grands Boulevards meet and is at the centre of a rhombus formed by four roads named after composers and librettists and is surrounded by rich and regular façades.

The Garnier Palace, a glamorous and imposing building, symbol of the reign of Napoleon III, is therefore in the centre of Paris in front of the famous «Café de la Paix».

The accomplishment of this monument was given to Charles Garnier in 1860 following a competition. He built a masterpiece which, for a long time, was taken as an example for theatres all over the world.

He was able to harmonise, in this gigantic monument of 11000 mq, the best styles and materials, and in a certain sense created a Napoleon III style, reflected by the taste of that period for pleasure and luxury: he created the building which is, without doubt, the richest of the century and also the most original.

The main façade expresses the monumentality of the building. The raised ground floor has

Theatre of the Opéra, edifice built between 1862 and 1875 on a project by the architect Charles Garnier.

Theatre of the Opéra: details.

Theatre of the Opéra: monument to C. Garnier.

Theatre of the Opéra at night.

Theatre of the Opéra: the big stairways in the entrance and the show hall.

a series of statues and groups, framed by low arcades. «La danse» (the dance) by Carpeaux (the original is to be found at the Louvre) is certainly the most noteworthy group due to its grace, harmony and luminosity.

The ground floor is surmounted by a palladian loggia where there is the foyer, and is supported by 16 twin columns, in red Bavarian stone, surmounted by bull's eyes with busts of musicians in golden bronze. The whole ends in a richly sculptured attic and behind this are mosaic medallions. The dome covered with glazed bronze is crowned by an Apollo with a lyre.

The interior, abundantly decorated with gilding, bronzes, marble, mosaics and crystals, is characterized by the gigantic staircase formed of curves and counter curves, with steps in white marble and onyx balustrades. It leads to the noble floor of the first class boxes of the foyer, a meeting place for the whole of Paris.

The hall itself, of less importance, seems to be planned both for the procession of the spectators and for the stage.

Under the gigantic chandelier the purple and gold seats are spread, they match the ceiling which Chagall painted in 1964 inspired by nine operas or ballets created from the music of Wagner, Berlioz, Mozart, Ravel, Debussy, Mussorgski, Adam, Tciaikovski and Stravinski.

Although it cannot contain more than 2200 spectators, the Opéra is and will always be the most important lyrical theatre of Paris.

PALAIS-ROYAL

Palais Royal: detail of the fountain.

The Royal Palace, which is today the seat of the Conseil d'Etat (Council of State) and of the Ministère de la Culture (Ministry of Culture), was a very animated place in Paris. Subsequently, having been neglected in spite of its peaceful garden, it was rediscovered with the opening and arrangement of the courtyard on the Buren side. In 1624, Cardinal Richelieu bought the ex hôtel of the Marquioness de Rambouillet in the quarter of Saint-Honoré and also the surrounding land, to build a luxurious palace.

The palace was planned in 1629 by the architect Jacques Lemercier. In 1642 Richelieu died there and bequeathed it to King Louis XIII: in this way it became the Palais-Royal. Anne d'Austria lived there with her two children as did Louis the Great and Philippe d'Orléans. Philippe d'Orléans went to live there when he became Regent and so the Palais-Royal became a theatre for his amusements.

After a fire in 1763, the nephew of the Regent had the façade on the courtyard of Contant d'Ivry rebuilt.

Duke Louis Philippe d'Orléans, who later became Philippe Egalité, decided to carry out an enormous property operation in order to pay his debts and had the garden built around the palace. He also had the ground floor of the building turned into galleries and shops. He summoned the aid of the architect Victor Louis who confined the garden with a double archade.

Imposing Corinthian pillars rise to the sculp-

Palais Royal: two views of the fountain and gardens.

tured gables of the windows of the noble floor. Between the 2nd courtyard and the gardens, the galleries of the building are connected to the archade.

The Palais Royal has now become a very popular quarter and is also a meeting place for artists. Under the archades you can find famous cafés such as the «Café du Foy», in the Galerie de Montpensier, where in the 13th July 1789 Camille Desmoulins incited the population to war.

The Duke d'Orléans was beheaded during the revolution and his palace became national property.

Under the Restauration the new Duke d'Orléans, the future Louis Philippe, restored the Palais Royal and transformed it. The architect Fontaine completed the main body of the 2nd courtyard and surrounded the encircling buildings with terraces. The Valois wing was completely restored and the interior was deco-

Pictures of Palais Royal.

rated. The d'Orleans gallery which connects the two wings was substituted by a normal wooden gallery and was lighted by a vaulted window.

The palace was invaded ard destroyed in 1848, then it was burnt down in 1871 under the Commune. Its restoration lasted from 1872 till 1876.

The main façade, consisting of a central part and two projecting wings, faces the Place du Palais Royal. A vaulted passage opens onto the double colonnade which leads to the garden. Under the galleries which run along the length of the garden are strange art, antiquarian and editorial curiosity shops.

Since 1986 the Cour d'Honneur (Court of Honour) has once more given rise to discussions over its arrangement. In fact in July 1985 Buren's project was chosen, on one hand with the aim of prohibiting the entry of cars which used it as a car park, and on the other to combine modern art with that of the past.

Therefore taking the colonnade of the d'Orléans gallery as reference, Buren planned lines which cross and delimit squares. At the centre of each of these and in the axis of the columns of the d'Orléans gallery is a cut off column. Here the desire to make the project form part of the architectonical composition of the Palais-Royal which is essentially linear, repetitive and woven can be seen.

All the columns have the same circumference as those of the galleries of Palais-Royal and are lined with vertical black and white stripes; however they can be both at ground level or reach a height of 3.19 m. The reticulated work is interrupted by two moats which cross each other at right angles. The illumination is also very important: at the ground intersection of every line of the reticular a beam of light also permits the continuation of this geometry by night. The moats are illuminated by a luminous line coming from under the wire netting, which lights the water and the underground columns.

Eglise (church) Saint-Roch.

ÉGLISE SAINT-ROCH

This church is among the most important classical religious buildings in Paris. It was built in the 18th century in this quarter, which was part of the parish of Saint-Germain-l'Auxerrois in order to keep pace with the increase of population.

The project was by Jacques Lemercier, the architect of the Sorbonne and the Val de Grâce, the foundation stone was laid by Louis XIV in 1653.

The death of Lemercier and the lack of funds delayed work for 40 years. Only the transept and choir were finished in 1660. Chapels were built in line with the apse to the detriment of the nave which was only started in 1719. It was finished in 1735 by Robert de Cotte and his son and the church was consecrated in 1740.

The façade, raised by a wide staircase, superimposes Doric and Corinthian orders. The interior is measured by large arches surmounted by a simple frieze. The particularity of this church consists of the alignment of the three chapels to which, in perspective, the altars are connected.

The chapel of the Virgin, with a circular base, was designed by Jules Hardouin-Mansart and covered with a dome decorated with an Assumption (XVIII); its side naves lead to the Communion Chapel decorated in a Corinthian style. Behind these two chapels is the third, the Calvary Chapel, constructed from the designs by Falconet, which contains a crucifix 2 m high.

His fame is due to a large number of funerary works of art, carried out by important sculptors of the 17th and 18th centuries. Famous men were buried there and often have a bust on their tomb, work of a famous sculptor. We can admire the bust of Magnard, work of Lemoyne, the statue of Cardinal Dubois by Coustou, Saint-Francis de Sales by Fajou and the valuable bust of Le Nôtre by Coysevox.

The church is also decorated with paintings la mort de Saint Louis (the death of Saint-Louis) by Coypel, la Présentation au Temple (The Presentation) and le Triomphe de Mardoché (the Triumph of Mardoch) by Restout.

PLACE DES VICTOIRES

This is the first square dedicated to Louis XIV. It was created by Maréchal de la Feuillade in gratitude to the king. He was ruined with the construction of this square.

The arrangement of the square was given to Jules Mansart. It has a circular shape with uniform buildings covered with pillars.

No adjoining road is aligned with another, in such a way as to form a kind of open air hall to display the royal statue to the full. The statue was ordered from the sculptor Desjardins and inaugurated in 1686. Louis XIV was represented standing, dressed in his coronation mantle, in the act of crushing a three headed dog (the triple alliance); various allegories decorated the whole.

Under the revolution the statue of the king was melted and substituted, in 1806, with an effigy of Desaix, represented in the nude according to ancient art. Due to this fact it gave rise to criticism and was melted in 1815.

The equestrian statue we can see today is of the Sun King sculptured by Bosio in 1882.

The opening of rue Etienne Marcel in 1883 has changed the tidy, closed disposition of the square as the rebuilding of buildings which break the regularity imposed by Jules Hardouin-Mansart.

Place de la Victoire.

Place de la Victoire: equestrian monument to the Roi Soleil.

Place de la Victoire.

THE BIBLIOTHÈQUE NATIONALE

The National Library contains one of the greatest collections of books in the world. It has been enriched with a copy of every book published in France since 1537. Originally the building was the Hôtel de Tubeuf; it was enlarged by Mansart for Cardinal Mazarino who adorned it with numerous paintings. When he died the hotel returned first to the crown and then to the national library. There are severe regulations for visits.

Palais Mazarin (with the fountain by Visconti and Pradier), seat of the National Library (square Louvois).

QUARTIER DU LOUVRE

SAINT-GERMAIN-L'AUXERROIS, RUE DE RIVOLI, THE LOUVRE. This quarter, from time to time preferred by kings, by artists or left in abandonment, is full of memories, such as the massacre of Saint-Barthélemy in 1572 or the fire at the Tuileries lit by the population in 1871, but it is also a place where there were important weddings and a brilliant intellectual and courtesan life. In this way the life of the quarter depended on the king's choice of residence.

Equestrian statue of Joan d'Arc erected in Place des Pyramides.

Church of Saint-Germain-l'Auxerrois: on the left of the bell tower the Town Hall of the I arrondissement.

The bell tower of the church of Saint-Germain-l'Auxerrois.

Below: Rue de Rivoli.

ÉGLISE SAINT-GERMAIN-L'AUXERROIS

When kings lived in the castle of the Louvre, the church of Saint-Germain-l'Auxerrois was the royal parish church. The present building, a sanctuary of the 8th century, is the valuable result of 5 centuries of architecture: the bell tower is Romanic, the ornate gothic choir was altered during the Renaissance, the nave and the arcade are shining gothic.

RUE DE RIVOLI

The first part of rue de Rivoli, between place de la Concorde and place du Palais-Royal, was opened under Napoleon I. From an architectural point of view it is the most interesting, ennobled by arcades. Today it is a beautiful gallery of shops. In 1848 it was lengthened until it reached rue de Sévigné.

THE LOUVRE

The royal palace is fruit of eight centuries. The fortress of the Louvre, against the ramparts of the right bank, was founded by King Philippe Auguste at the end of the 12th century to protect the western part of Paris. In the 14th century the wall of defence was removed annulling the original function of the castle; Charles V restored it and left the Cité palace

The Clock of the Louvre.

to settle there. The architect R. du Temple mainly constructed the North and East wings on the opposite side of the 13th century barrages. His gardens and library were famous. Only the foundations in the south-west corner of the present courtyard remain of this primitive Louvre. Two archeological cripts have been excavated and will be opened to the public in 1988.

During the Renaissance, Francis I had the keep and the west and south wings demolished. They were rebuilt according to the taste of the period by the architect Pierre Lescot, this work was started in 1546. Work was continued under Henry II, Charles X and Henry III. The sculptured decoration is by Jean Goujon.

After the death of Henry II at the Tournelles in 1559, his wife Cathrine de Medici had the Tuileries palace built by Philibert de l'Orme in order to banish the sad memory. Henry XIII connected it to the Louvre by the Petite Galérie and the Grande Galérie along the Seine (about 442 m long). In 1624, under Louis XIII, Lemercier built the «pavillon de l'horloge» (the clock pavilion) and lengthened it with a renaissance style wing. Louis XIV had the last gothic wing demolished and continued with the construction of the Cour Carrée (square courtyard), flanking it on the east by the «colonnade» by Claude Perrault. Under Napoleon I, Percier and Fontaine finished the Cour and started a wing in symmetry with the gallery of Henry IV and finished place du Carrousel. Napoleon III had the «grand dessein» (great project) carried out which was sketched at the time of Louis XIII: Baron Haussmann demolished the quarters between the two palaces and finished the wing which skirts rue de Rivoli. By this time the Tuileries palace was united to the Louvre. However a few years later the Tuileries was set on fire during a revolt of the Commune (1871).

Architectural description. The present buildings are the work or 4 different centuries, however they have a certain unity of style because the successive architects always adapted their style to the initial renaissance building by P. Lescot and J. Goujon.

Therefore, when Cardinal Richelieu, a great builder, decided to give a royal magnificence to the palace, he had Lemercier carry out the clock pavilion and the continuation of the west wing, faithfully reproducing the already existing work.

Half of the south wing and the east and north wings, started during the century of Louis XIV and finished under Napoleon III, betray however a more classical style.

The «colonnade». At the beginning of the reign of Louis XIV work was started on the Louvre because Colbert wanted the King to live there. The eastern façade of the «Cour Carrée» needed particular attention and a competition of architecture was announced.

The jury, presided over by Colbert, chose Bernini, the famous architect in the pope's service. His Italian baroque style perplexed the French who then realized that they had their own artistic tendency, the artist was dismissed with great scandal, and the French turned deliberately towards a French style. The project adopted therefore, consists of a manifest of French Classicism, which unites baroque grandeur with the order inherited from the Renaissance. In fact Claude Perrault decided on a theatrical type of colonnade. These innovations in style also took on the aspect of a technical wager due to the dimensions of the columns, the highest which had ever been constructed until that date. The solution was an iron framework.

Subsequent destinations of the Louvre. Under Philippe Auguste it was a fortified keep, arsenal and royal treasury then the castle of the Louvre became the pleasant abode of Charles Vth. Francis Ist brough it out of the state of abandonment into which it had fallen, this was a prelude to the intense courtisan life of which it was the framework in the 17th century. As the court was then moved to Versailles, the Louvre was rented to some artists. From 1737 till 1848 the Exhibitions of the Académie Royale de Peinture et Sculpture (Royal Academy of Painting and Sculpture) were held in the «Salon Carré» (Square Hall).

During the reign of Louis XV the «élite» launched the idea of opening a small museum at the Louvre. On the 10th August 1793, the Grande Galérie presented a combination of paintings and ancient works of art to the public. The plunder of the Napoleonic wars formed an exceptional collection of works of art, organized by Vivant Denon. When they were restituted in 1815 they were replaced by other works which were subsequently displayed in the Cour Carrée and then in the north wing of Napoleon III. Today the Louvre museum is one of the richest in the world. From the Pavillon de Flore to the Pavillon de Marsan the Louvre stretches for 1700 km, multiplied by its many floors.

Grand Louvre Project. Born as a keep, the Louvre was transformed into a country house and lastly into an important palace, «grand Dessein» (great plan) carried on throughout three centuries (from the time of Louis XIII to the IIIrd Republic). The Grand Louvre project, decided in 1981, is part of this plan because it destined the entire palace to become a mu-

A foreshortening of the Louvre and the gardens of Tuileries.

The Louvre: partial view of the Palace and gardens of Tuileries.

Window, quai du Louvre.

seum. In this way the collections will be displayed again and space for receptions and services will be created. In the Cour Napoléon, a glass pyramid conceived by I.M. Pei will cover and show the central area of the entrance, permitting both the reorganization of the space inside the palace and the opening of the museum to the town. Added to this project are archeological excavations and a restoration campaign which are to the benefit of Cour Carrée, the Galérie d'Apollon and some collections. The project will be completed towards 1998.

The present collections in the museum. The rich collections in the museum are divided into 6 «départements» (sections): ancient Egyptian, ancient oriental, ancient Greek and Roman, paintings, sculpture and works of art.

The collections of the ancient Egyptian section evoke the entire history of the pharaons of the Tinitian period (towards 3000 B.C.), with, for example, the «stele of the serpent king», un-

til the «Basse Epoque» (5th and 4th centuries B.C.). Among the main works are the fascinating «squatting scribe» (Ancient Empire), the reconstruction of a small chapel of the Vth Dynasty, the colossal bust of Amenophis IVth, a masterpiece of the Amarnian period, sumptuous jewels of Rameses II, numerous holy statues, etc.

The section of oriental antiquities is dedicated to Mesopotamia, Persia, Phoenicia and Palestine, ancient civilizations of the Near and Far East.

The Greek antiquities include the geometric period (1050-720 B.C.) with the frontal and austere «Dame d'Auxerre»; the archaic period (620-480 B.C.) with the original head of a knight called «Rampin», the classicism (half 5th-4th centuries) illustrated by sculptures from the Parthénon. The Hellenistic period (3rd-1st centuries B.C.) is superbly represented by the «Victory of Samothrace», of the 1st century, a power-

Watteau, an artist of the beginning of the 17th century, is the author of «Gilles», a mysterious and malinconic figure. The consecration of Napoleon I, which took place on 2nd December 1804, carried out by Pope Pius VII at Notre-Dame-de-Paris, is immortalized in the huge painting by David which is majestically carried out.

The Italian school is widely represented, from the Primitives to the 18th century: there can be found the main works of Cimabue, Giotto, Beato Angelico, Mantegna, Leonardo da Vinci, Raffaello, the Venetians of the 16th century, Caravaggio, Tiepolo, Guardi, etc. «The Gioconda» said to be «the most beautiful painting in the world», is of Monna Lisa Gherardini, wife of the Florentine Del Giocondo, hence the nickname. In this work, Leonardo da Vinci (1452-1519), has created a subtle unity of tone through the use of light and shade, ingenious conclusion of pictorical research of the Florentine 15th century art.

Among the many paintings of the Flemish and Dutch schools are: «The Madonna of Chancelor Rolin» by Van Eyck, «The beggars» by Brueghel, the 21 compositions by Rubens illustrating the life of Maria de Medici, «The pilgrims of Emmaus» by Rembrandt, «The Lacemaker» by Vermeer.

Paintings of great value are also numbered among the Spanish, English and German schools. We can mention «the Crucifix» by El Greco, «A Conversation in a Park» by Gainsborough and a self portrait in charcoal by Dürer.

The sculpture section includes French art from the Romanesque period to the 19th century, with a Renaissance masterpiece, the «Diana of Aneto», statues by Puget, portraits by Houdon, «Eros kissing Psyche» by Canova. Among the Italians we can find Michelangelo («The Slaves»), Donatello and B. Cellini.

The Apollo gallery is the most sumptuous part of the object of art section due to its decoration by Le Brun and the magnificent «Crown Jewels», the ornaments for the consecration of the kings of France, etc., of which it is the coffer.

ful winged woman in impetuous movement which, placed on the prow of a stone galley, commemorated a naval victory. As far as the Venus de Milo is concerned (2nd century), discovered in 1830 on the island of Milo, it is a masterpiece of Greek statuary due to the purity of its form.

Some exhibits of the Etruscan civilization are also worth mentioning, such as the Cerveteri sarcophagus.

The Roman antiquities are, for the most part, dedicated to the Imperial period (27 B.C. to the 3rd century A.D.): there are beautiful statues of Caligola, Messalina, Nero, Trajan, Hadrian and Marcus Aurelius.

The section of paintings is very rich and in particular the part which concerns western art of the 16th, 17th and 18th centuries. Works of after 1848 are at the d'Orsay museum and the 20th century is exhibited at the National Museum of Modern Art and at the G. Pompidou Centre.

The 16th century French school is represented by the veracity of the royal portraits by Clouet and the Fontainebleau School with «Gabrielle d'Estrées et la Maréchale de Blagny», a painting which shows the two sisters in the bath, in which the beautiful Gabrielle, official mistress of King Henry IV, shows off her pregnancy with the conventional gesture of expressing a drop of milk. The 17th century collection includes the official portrait of Louis XIV by Rigaud.

Above: decorative detail.

The Louvre, comprehensive view.

The Carrousel and detail of the Louvre.

The plastic model of the Pyramid.

The erecting yard and the pyramid structures.

1. *Egyptian art.* **Sitting scribe.**
   Dating back to around 2450 B.C. this work is made of painted calcareous material. The scribe, 53 cm tall, represents one of the masterpieces of the Egyptian art and was found in 1850 during excavations in Saqqârah.

2-3. Rooms containing works of Roman and Egyptian art.

4. The grand staircase leading to the room of the Victory of Samothrace.

5. *Hellenistic art.* **Victory of Samothrace.**
   It is beyond doubt one of the most important and extraordinary works of the all Hellenistic plastic art. Found in Samothrace in 1863 the Victory has neither head nor arms. The statue made of Parian marble and 2.75 mts high, is represented as standing on the ship which around 190 B.C. led the Rhodian fleet to victory against Antiochus IIIrd.

1. *Hellenistic art:* **Venus de Milo.**

This statue, just over two metres high, belongs to the Hellenistic age (end of the 2nd century B.C.); it is almost certainly copied from an original by Prassiteles. Discovered in 1820 on the island of Milos in the Ciclades, it has become the model of Greek feminine beauty.

2. *Hellenistic art:* **exhibition room showing the Venus de Milo.**

3. *Roman art:* **exhibition room of the sculptures.**

4. **Michelangelo Buonarroti.** (1475-1564). *The Slave.*

Executed between 1513 and 1520 for the basement of the mausoleum of Julius II and donated in 1550 to Henry II by the Florentine Roberto Strozzi, the sculpture ended up in the Louvre at the time of the revolution.

1. *Mesopotamian art:*
Statue of Judea.

Judea was Prince of the Sumerian city of Lagash at around 2,000 B.C. His reign represented a period of peace and prosperity as well as an extraordinary cultural and artistic «renaissance» as it appears well documented in the several sculpted portraits and in the many inscriptions which represent the most wide-ranging and valuable texts in the Neo-Sumerian language. In the series of statues that come mainly from Tellos, Judea is represented as either seated or standing but always in a religious pose in the act of prayer.

In these times the figure of the dignitary summed up the political and religious power of the city. The statue represented here is one of the most significant, not only for its beauty, but also for the religious sense it expresses. It is made of black, volcanic rock, and stands one and a half metres high, and Judea is wearing the characteristic Persian sheepskin hat and, over his shoulders, a simple coat. It belongs to the high dynastic period of the 3rd century B.C.

2. *Egyptian art:* **Queen Karomana.**

Statue in bronze finished in gold belonging to the third intermediate period (10th-6th centuries B.C.).

3. *Assyrian art:* **Bearded Warrior.**

4. *Persian art:* **Winged Ibex.** (5th century B.C.).

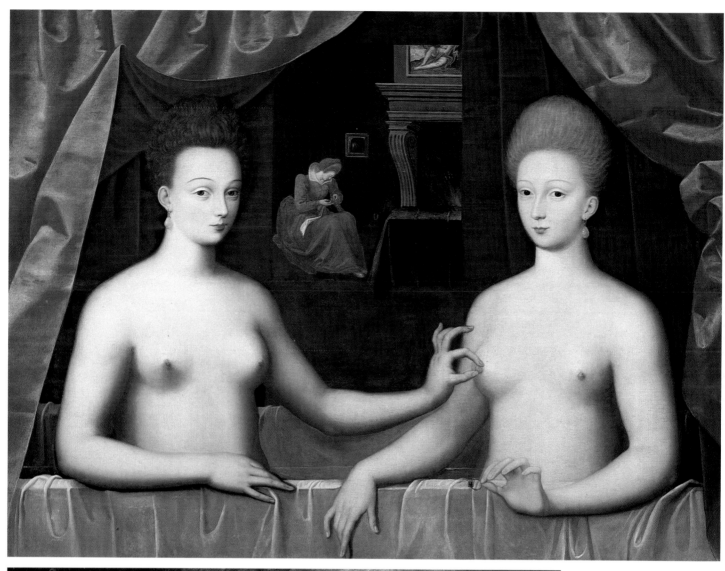

◀ **Nicolas Poussin**
(1594-1665) *Bacchanalia*

One of the best inter-
preters of the renewed classic ideals of the 17th century, founded under the insignia of order, clarity and simplicity, Poussin was the ad-
vocate of a poetic vision, in
contradiction to a profound
intellectual meditation, in
which the sensibility of
Venetian Colourism blends
with the epic dimension of
the classical Raphaelite
ideal. The Bacchanalia, incorporated in 1665 into the
collection of the Duke
Richelieu after which it
passed into the hands of
Louis XIV, dates from
around 1627-1628 and, by
its close affinity with Titian's *Andrii* (Prado, Madrid),
very probably illustrates a
passage from Flostrato that
describes the island of An-
dro, on which, courtesy of
Bacchus, the wine flows in
rivers.

School of Fontainebleau. Anonymous. *Gabrielle d'Estrées and one of her sisters.*

The work, dating from around 1594, recalls, by its deliberately archaic features, the style of the first School of Fontainebleau which began to define itself with original characteristics from 1528 at the time when Francis I, wishing to re-establish his own prestige after the defeat at Pavia, asked Rosso Fiorentino to decorate the royal apartments of the castle, situated at the edge of the Forest of Bievre. Thanks to the works of the Italian and of the other artists who collaborated with him or continued the works: Primaticcio, Niccolò dell'Abate, Cellini ..., Fontainebleau became one of the main centres of the burgeoning of Mannerism, which had become the international style. The painting reproduced here shrewdly depicts, through the importance given to the studied rhythm of the long arms and the beautiful and graceful gestures, the ideal of the worn-out and sensual elegance that inspired the art of Fontainebleau.

Nicolas Poussin. *Autumn*

The painting belongs to a cycle dedicated to the four seasons and was executed between 1660-1664 for the Duke of Richelieu. Poussin expresses the feeling of a universal harmony that unites the fortunes of humanity with the laws of nature giving life to a wonderful synthesis between nature and history and to a most profound meditation on the stages of human life.

Hyacinthe Rigaud. *Louis XIV* ▶

Rigaud was one of the official portrait painters most sought after by the French and European aristocracy of his time. He was Louis XIV's painter, par excellence, in the same way that Van Dyck, who was his favourite master and who inspired his work, had been for Charles I of England. With a vivacious pictorial touch and a dazzling chromaticity, Rigaud shrewdly interpreted the need for the scenic splendour of baroque portrait painting of which the present portrait constitutes one of the most eloquent and remarkable examples.

François Boucher, (1703-1770). *Country Feast* ▲

Influenced by the style of Watteau, Boucher was the favourite painter of the French court and aristocracy of his time to the extent that he became «first royal painter», partly thanks to the protection of Madame de Pompadour who had been his pupil and of whom he painted several sensual portraits. Boucher was the exquisite interpreter of the rococo taste and of the society which had produced it. The elegant, bucolic idyll reproduced here with its mawkishness, its coquettishness and the sense of languid abandonment recalls the senses that prevail in it and constitutes a perfect example of the playful ethereality of late baroque painting.

◀ Jean-Honoré Fragonard. *The Letter*

A pupil of Boucher and profoundly influenced by his example, Fragonard was the major exponent of rococo art which was nevertheless beginning to decline. Through the sensuality, both vivid and ethereal, that he managed to conflate, he was the supreme interpreter of the genre of the bucolic idyll from which the taste of the elegant society of his time provided so much pleasure. *The Letter* constitutes a superb example of the gossamer and light gracefulness of the artist's work.

Jean-Antoine Watteau (1684-1721). *Gilles and another four characters of the commedia dell'arte*

The theatre and the world of masquerade constitute one of the main sources of inspiration of Watteau's painting. He was one of the greatest artists of the French baroque and was incomparable in the rendering of entranced atmospheres corruscating with golden lights. The painting reproduced here probably composed between 1717-1719 presents us, in the character of Gilles, with and unforgettable representation of sadness, one of the most intense ever depicted in the history of art.

Eugène Delacroix (1798-1863). *Liberty Guiding the People*

Profound renovator of the modern pictorial language, Delacroix is the highest interpreter of French Romanticism, the artist who, better than anyone else, knew how to express the creative freedom of which he was the best and most original figure. With his work, contemporary painting discovered the heroism of passion and the fire of an imagination that overwhelms and recreates everything under the power of the most intense subjectivity. The painting reproduced here is one of the most famous and celebrated of the works of Delacroix, who painted it shortly after the revolutionary movements of July 1830 and exhibited it at the Salon of 1831, where it was purchased by Louis-Philippe for the Musée Royal. It is one of the first political compositions of modern painting and it demonstrates the interest with which Romanticism looked at and participated in the acts of contemporary life.

Jean-Auguste-Dominique Ingres. (1780-1867). *The Great Odalisque*

Ingres, a pupil of David, is the greatest and most coherent exponent of 19th century classicism, upholder of a pictorial vision based on the search for formal perfection attainable through the incomparable supremacy of drawing. *The Great Odalisque*, one of the favourite themes in the imagination of the artist, was painted in Rome in 1814, commissioned by Caroline Murat, and constitutes one of the finest examples of the classicist pictorial ideal and its yearning for giving life to «timeless» art governed by the laws of equilibrium, harmony and perfection.

▲

Jacques-Louis David. (1748-1825). *Napoleon, the first Consul*

Incomparable protagonist of the French Neo-Classicism and one of the finest interpreters of the profound change in taste that took place in Europe during the last twenty years of the 1700's promoted by the re-discovery of the antique, David gave painting the character of a planned ethical finality coherently and tenaciously followed from the times of his revolutionary commitment until his last days spent, after the fall of Napoleon and the Restoration, in exile in Brussels. The portrait of Napoleon was begun in 1799 and remained unfinished. It evidences, while maintaining an 18th century La Tour style, the burgeoning of a new passionate sentiment that anticipates the romantic sensitivity.

Jacques-Louis David. *The Coronation* ▶

The canvas, of enormous proportions, was painted between 1805-1807 and represents the ceremony of the coronation of Josephine by Napoleon which took place in Nôtre-Dame on December 2nd, 1804. For this painting David drew many sketches from the actual event, submitting them to the Emperor for approval and accepting from him more than one suggestion. The result is not at all encumbered by the long genesis that prepared the execution of the painting. On the contrary, it surprises by the fidelity and freshness through which the visual reality is rendered and by the intense and vibrant luminosity of the chromatism which already anticipates the colourist taste of the romantics.

Tiziano Vecellio. (c. 1490-1576). *Madonna of the Rabbit*

An artist of prime significance in the history of Italian Renaissance painting, Titian interpreted, more profoundly than any other artist, the refulgent colour of the Venetian tradition in the 1500's which becomes, in his work, sumptuously expressive, by virtue of its intense sensuality, and palpitates with vitality. In the *Madonna of the Rabbit*, painted in around 1530, the dense and enveloping structure creates the perfect atmosphere for the revelation of an imminent sunset that reverberates from its own light in the whole composition and gives it a subtle intimacy.

◀ **Raphael Sanzio.** (1483-1520). *The Holy Family with Saint Elizabeth, Saint John and Two Angels*

The greatest interpreter of Renaissance values, especially in his Roman period from 1508 until his death, Raphael knew how to synthesize beautifully, in a grandiose idealisation, the renewed prestige of the classical tradition, of which he was the leading exponent, with the spiritual message of the Christian faith. The work reproduced here, signed and dated on the Virgin's gown, was executed at the moment when he was decorating the Vatican Stanze in June, 1518, and Leo X sent it, together with another one of the master's paintings, to Francis I. Painted with the assistance of his apprentices, the work stands out by the strength of its compositional synthesis and by its unique effects of colour and light with which the artist experimented.

Leonardo da Vinci. (1452-1519). *La Gioconda*

The painting, which constitutes one of the most famous and widely reproduced works in the history of art, is considered to be, according to the testimony of Vasari, the portrait of Monna Lisa who was born in Florence in 1479 and had married the Marquis of Giocondo, a Florentine nobleman, in 1495. Leonardo transported the painting to Milan when he moved to the Lombard capital in 1482. From here it was taken to France where Francis I purchased it from Leonardo's executor after the death of the artist. By Vasari's account, Leonardo had worked on it for four years without managing to complete it, but the painting, which can be dated at around 1503-1506, appears to be definitely and beautifully finished in regard to the quality of the unity between figure and landscape.

Diego Velázquez. (1599-1660). *Portrait of Mariana de Austria*

Francisco de Goya. (1746-1828). *The Marchioness of Solana*

One of the greatest interpreters of 17th century naturalism, Velázquez, from the very beginning, oriented his own work towards a style inspired by Caraveggesque models, both in the choice of motifs of the popular life and in the use of great chiaroscuro contrasts that underlined the plastic strength of the figures. Nominated court painter thanks to the benevolence and the support of the powerful Conde de Olivares, Velásquez ascended rapidly to a position of unquestioned supremacy, influencing, in a decisive way, the transformation of the artistic taste of the Spanish court. The painting reproduced here is a lifesize portrait of the German Emperor, Ferdinand III, and of his wife, Maria, the sister of Philip IV of Spain. Mariana had been betrothed to the infant, Baltasar Carlos, but, when he died prematurely, she was married to her uncle who had become a widower. The wedding took place in 1649 and Velázquez, who could not attend the ceremony because he was absent from Madrid, painted the portrait on his return, towards the end of 1651.

Starting from the 18th century tradition, Goya was influenced in his youth by the works of Tiepolo and of Mengs. After the example of Velázquez, for whom he held a profound admiration, Goya soon departed from traditional art and moved towards a freedom of observation and execution unequalled in his own time. Through this he gave life to an artistic creation freed from any academic constraints and engaged in witnessing the dramatic and disturbing events of his time. This portrait, which is considered one of the masterpieces of Goya's portrait painting, is that of Maria Rita Barrenechea y Morante, wife of the Count of Carpio. Executed at around 1792, the picture belongs to the so-called «grey-period» of the artist and attests to the extraordinary quality of Goya's painting which is capable of amazingly fine brush strokes like the ones that can be seen in the impalpable rendering of the veil and of the wonderful pink bow in her hair.

MARIA ERGO ACCEPIT LIBRAM VNGETI NARDI PISTICI PDIOSE ET VXIT PEDES IHV

Rogier Van der Weiden. (c. 1400-1464). ▲
Braque Triptych: The Magdalene

One of the greatest interpreters of Flemish painting of the 15th century, the artist, who was a pupil of Robert Campin whose influence is recognizable in the first works of the painter, made contact with Italian art which he encountered directly during his sojourn in Italy and which left a profound impression on his style, attenuating the primitive dramatization in favour of more moderate and refined spatial scansions. The work reproduced here is painted on the right wing of the small, portable triptych commissioned by Catherine of Brabant in memory of her husband, Jehan Braque, who died in 1452, and belongs to the moment of the greatest equilibrium of the art of Rogier in which we can recognise a certain reflection of the painting of Beato Angelico.

Hans Memling. (1435-1494). *A Mystical Marriage of St. Catherine of Alexandria*

A pupil of Rogier Van der Weiden, the artist, who gave life to a most fecund production, made a complex synthesis of the lessons of the greatest Flemish artists who lived and worked before him. He knew how to blend the styles of Van Eyck, Van der Weiden, Bouts and Van der goes, together with a sprinkling of Italianism. The work reproduced here is a fusion of the theme of mystical marriage and of the representation of the «hortus conclusus», symbol of the purity of the Madonna and the virgins who surround her.

Jan van Eyck. (1390-1441). *The Madonna of* ▶
Chancellor Rolin

Van Eyck was the initiator of the new Flemish painting, now completely detached from the Gothic tradition of the Netherlands, and the creator of a pictorial vision, prodigious in its ability to render details through infinite gradations of light and innumerable reflections. The painting reproduced here probably in around 1436 depicts Nicolas Rolin, Chancellor of Borgogna, who had an important role in the court of Philip the Good, praying before the Virgin Mary.

◄**Frans Hals.** (c. 1580-1666). *The Gypsy Woman*

Portrait painter, among the greatest of the century, Frans Hals is with Velázquez and Rembrandt, the creator of modern, pictorial language through which, by the example of his style made with rapid and irregular brush strokes, he learned not to hide his distinctly recognizable technique. Because of his modernity and revolutionary style, Hals was almost completely unknown by successive generations and was re-discovered, as a revelation, only in the 19th century when his work constituted an important point of reference for artists such as Courbet and Manet. *The Gypsy Woman*, which can be dated between 1628-1630, is a decisively eloquent example of how Hals' technique, through the back and forth movement of brush strokes, knows how to grasp the immediacy of the visual and suggests the instantaneousness of life in its strength of appearance.

◄ Pieter Paul Rubens.
(1577-1640). *The Flemish Country Feast*

Through a complex process of assimilation of Italian artistic culture of the 1500's and early 1600's, thanks to which he gradually learned Titian's lessons on chromatism and Caravaggio's luminosity, Rubens arrived at a cosmopolitan, baroque vision which exercised an enormous influence on the course of European painting, to which he opened the horizon of a new richness of composition of grandiose monumentality and of a vivid exhaltation of colour and forms of an extraordinary wealth. *The Feast*, which appears in the late work of the artist, between 1635-1637, reelaborates a typical topos of the Flemish pictorial tradition; that of the country feast already treated with incomparable results by the genius of Bruegel, the Elder.

Rembrandt van Rijn.
(1606-1669). *Self-Portrait*

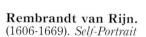

One of the greatest artists of all time, Rembrandt, after completing his humanist studies, began to dedicate himself to painting under the guidance of Pieter Lastman, a painter of Italianate culture. He lived during the most flourishing period of Dutch art which was maintained and encouraged by a rapidly rising merchant bourgeoisie. Sustained by a prodigious technical quality, Rembrandt's art, which was profused in painting as well as engraving, remains unrelated to the meticulously analytic realism of the contemporary genrepainting and to the pompous and passionate taste of the baroque style. He gave life to a profoundly interiorised representation of reality, extending it in order to understand the meaning and ultimate truth of existance. This extraordinary interrogation of the meaning of human life has produced an endless catalogue of works, consisting in his paintings, engravings and drawings, that reveals itsefl as a very compact whole shining with an identity and heroic passion and, at the same time, is anchored in the human participation in the episode of existence, anxious and tormented as well as intensely lived. The insistence with which Rembrandt repeated, during the course of his life, the motif of the self-portrait, to the point that it became the leitmotif of his whole work, is an extremely eloquent testimony of the artist's disposition to delve inside himself for the justifications for his own artistic creation. The work reproduced here, painted in 1633, when the artist was just over twenty-eight years of age and had recently finished such a masterpiece as *The Anatomy Lesson of Professor Nicolaas Tulp*, represents a painting of the highest quality that dealt with the individuation of the revealing significance of light, realizing one of the artist's main objectives which he achieved wonderfully in the masterpieces of his maturity and old age, such as *The Night Watch (1642), Bethsheba (1654), or The Night Guest of Claudio Civile (1661)*. In the present self-portrait, the light that suddenly brightens the face, making it stand out from the brown background, has always revealed strong dramatic evidence of the most hidden feelings of the soul and the most secret passions of man in Rembrandt's art.

Bronze sculpture by Rodin.

The gardens of Tuileries.

THE CARROUSEL

Between the two wings of the Louvre are the gardens of the Carrousel, named in remembrance of the equestrian parades which took place there to celebrate the birth of the Dauphin Louis XV (The Grand Carrousel of June 1662).

On the left, the Carrousel. Note in the foreground the obelisk of Place de la Concorde and the Arc de Triomphe.

Bronze sculptures by Rodin.

A small triumphal arch, a replica of the arch of Septimius Severus in Rome, was erected following the design of Percier and Fontaine to celebrate Napoleon's victories in the 1805 campaigns: Austerlitz, Ulm, etc.; originally it was the monumental entrance of the Tuileries palace.

The 4 horses from Saint-Mark's in Venice, emblems of power, were on top of the arch until 1815 when they were given back to the Venetians. The sculptor Bosio substituted them with a quadriga driven by a woman who represents the Restoration.

JARDIN DES TUILERIES

Towards 1560, when the Tuileries palace was built for Cathérine de Medici, a garden was also made. A century later the gardener transformed it into a «French style» garden. Around the superb perspective of the central avenue there are pools and flowerbeds, enlivened by geometrical decorations. The master is Le Nôtre, who became gardener of Louis XIV. Today this garden is still a place to wander for the Parisians. A rich collection of sculptures by Maillol (beginning of the 20th century) adorn its lawns.

At the end of the garden are the museums of the Orangerie and of the Jeu de Paume which contain temporary exhibitions.

THE HALLES - BEAUBOURG - QUARTER HÔTEL DE VILLE

In its renewed and contemporary alliance with the past, this quarter has known how to find its own identity and its own life.

A place of culture and amusement, from **place du Châtelet** *to the* **Bourse du Commerce**, *going past* **Hôtel de Ville**, *the Beaubourg quarter with the church of* **Saint-Merri** *and the les Halles with the church of* **Saint-Eustache**, *the ex «womb of Paris» is one of the first examples of the present reorganization of Paris.*

Place du Châtelet: detail of the column.

Fontaine du Châtelet: detail.

PLACE DU CHÂTELET

The square is flanked by two theatres built by Davioud in 1862: the «Théâtre du Châtelet» and the «Théâtre de la Ville». Their neo-renaissance furnishing hides a very modern interiors.

At the centre is the «du Châtelet» fountain (or «of Victory»), built in 1806 in memory of Napoleon's expedition to Egypt.

The place du Châtelet is situated on the site of the «Grand Châtelet», théâtre where the Police Office, torture chambers, prisons and the morgue were to be found.

It was destroyed in 1810.

TOUR SAINT-JACQUES

This is a rather unusual tower, which marks the end of the gothic period, and dominates the quarter from the height of its 52 m.

It is the bell tower of the ex church of Saint-Jacques «de la Boucherie» (of the Butchers) (called in this way because of its vicinity to the butchers near the Grand Châtelet), it was built in 1522 by Jean Felin and demolished during the revolution.

The tower had to be taken from its foundations when rue de Rivoli was opened; it was erected with a base to raise the difference of levels.

It was rented for a long time to an armourer who used it to make small shot for hunting: this was obtained by pouring molten lead from the top.

In the XIXth century having become the property of the Ville de Paris, it was restored. The ruined statues were reproduced, above all that of Saint-Jacques le Majeur, and the abaci were substitued with glass.

At the foot of the tower the first Paris square (square and garden) were made.

Place du Châtelet and, on the right, tower of St. Jacques.

HÔTEL DE VILLE

Equestrian statue of Etienne Marcel.

The square of the Hôtel de Ville, reserved in part for pedestrians, is situated between rue de Rivoli and the Seine, and is dominated by the imposing façade of Hôtel de Ville, which seems almost unreal in its whiteness, enhanced by the granite pavement, constructed over the car park in 1982.

This rather conventional place has been a very lively centre during the centuries.

The history of the «Mairie» (the Commune) goes back to Saint-Louis. At the head of the Commune administration there is a Rector of the merchants and four municipal magistrates.

From 1533 to 1628, where the Hôtel de Ville now stands, there was a palace built in Italian renaissance style. However the revolution confered it with a fundamental role. At the Hôtel de Ville, on the 17th July 1789, the king went under a series of crossed swords to kiss the tricolour cockade which had just been adopted: blue and red, the colours of the city of Paris, to which Lafayette had added white, the colour of the monarchy. Three years later it was the seat of the insurrectionary Commune.

In 1848, in the name of the great revolution of 1789, the provisional government was then installed at the Hôtel de Ville.

Then, at the end of the week of bloody repression in May 1871, it was reduced to a pile of smoking ruins at the hands of the inhabitants of Versailles. The reconstruction project was given to the architects Ballu and Deperthes in 1871. The immense façade of the 19th century has a renaissance appearance. The area is of about 13,000 square metres. The two large doors, flanked by the lateral pavillion, give access to the courtyards.

The smaller central door, is raised. On the balaustrade in front of it, the statues of Art and Science can be seen. The four façades are decorated with numerous statues of famous men who were born in Paris. The pediment supports the bell tower and is crowned by two statues of women holding the Paris coats of arms.

Inside, the luxurious staircase leads to the ball room and the reception saloon. The heavy rich decoration bears witness to the tastes of the last century (allegorical composition, tapestries, parquet floors impregnated with precious perfumes, chandeliers in Baccarat crystal). Among other things you can admire Rodin's bust of the Republic, statues by Daulon, frescos by Laurens and Puvis de Chavannes and scenes of Parisian life, work of the caricaturist Villette.

In 1977 the Parisians elected their first mayor Jacques Chirac; the counsillors met in a large saloon which was open to the public.

Regarding the square of the Hôtel de Ville,

Hôtel de Ville at night.

it was given this name in 1806. Before then, as it went down to the Seine, it was called «place de Grève» (pebbly Shore'Square). It was there that the unemployed workers met (from here the expression «faire grève», to strike, was born). It was in this square as well, from the 14th to the end of the 18th century that the executioners burned beheaded, and guillotined.

The 25th February 1848 Lamartine refused to recognise the red flag on this square.

The Republic was proclamed there on the 4th September 1870 and lastly, in 1944, General De Gaulle arrived there as victor.

On the left, fountain of Place de l'Hôtel de Ville.

Hôtel de Ville: comprehensive view.

Shot taken at night from the Pompidou Centre.

THE GEORGE POMPIDOU CENTRE

Pompidou Centre: detail of the ascending moving staircase.

Pompidou Centre: comprehensive view of the structure.

After the Eiffel tower, the George Pompidou center can boast of being the only one to have caused so many controversies.

Appreciated by some people, it is strongly criticized by others.

It is part of new quarter and for the greater part is reserved for pedestrians and is today considered to be the first contemporany building in Paris. It has become a centre of attraction, where an immense crowd mingles continually and often tarries on the square, forming small groups around a fire eater, a «chansonnier», a musician..., creating an animation which is reminiscent of medieval times.

It is the first project in the Semah operation programme which has been finished and it occupies the area of the «Beau Bourg» ex-esplanade, a name which was given ironically when it became the Halles unloading place. The audacious and ambitious initiative of building a center of modern art was of Georges Pompidou, President of the Republic in 1969.

The ideology of the seventies which thought that a museum should be opened to a vast num-

Pompidou Centre: panoramic view of Place G. Pompidou.

Pompidou Centre: the ground floor hall.

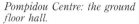

ber of the public in order to promote comparison, creativity and research was expressed with this building, which is open on an architectural plane both to the public and to artists, with exhibitions which steadily follow one after the other.

The project by the architects Renzo Piano and Richard Rogers was chosen in the international competition.

The building was started in 1972 and it was inaugurated in 1977. It is 166 m long, 60 m wide and 40 m high, it has immense areas in which the installations are functional and visible from the exterior on 5 floors, the characteristic escalator winds in a glass tube, which enlivens the façade with the movement of the crowd. The system of tubes, each with its own colour to show its function (red for circulation, green for water, blue for aeration, yellow for electricity), make the building picturesquely colourfull.

From the panoramic terrace you can enjoy a

Pompidou Centre: folk show (detail).

The great animated fountain.

Hôtel de Ville, Notre-Dame and Tour Saint-Jacques at night.

magnificent view of the roofs of the whole of Paris.

The Georges Pompidou Centre has become the heart of four important activities:

— *plastic art*, with the Great National Museum of Modern Art in which the collections of the Modern Art Museum (which was in avenue du President Wilson) and those of the National Centre of Contemporary Art are united and to which other donations have been added, such as works by Kandinskji. There are also different artistic trends represented there, from fauvism, to cubism, to surrealism. To the abstract, until we come to contemporary art in which different international currents meet;

— *the public library*, as a place for promoting reading: this contains thousands of books, divided between three floors, which already seem too small to contain them; beside them are the videos;

— *industrial aesthetics*, represented by the Industrial Creation Centre. This includeds numerous original exibitions which are intended to stimulate the visitor to have a critical vision of his surroundings. Therefore the exhibitions concern both architecture and urbanistics and also consumer goods, comic strips, posters and any other means of visual communication;

— *music*: for this the «Institut de Recherche et de Coordination Acoustique Musicale» (Institute of Acoustical Musical Research and Coordination) was created. This is a real underground laboratory directed by Pierre Boulez, in which musical creation is promoted by exceptional means.

At the foot of the Centre, in front of the church of Saint-Merri there is the first great animated modern fountain in Paris, this fountain is also very colourful. It was created by N. de Saint-Phalle and J. Tinguely in 1983 and dedicated to Stravinski: it represents an allegory of the orchestra moving around the conductor.

On the right the big clock.

QUARTIER DE L'HORLOGE

This is the ex «îlot Saint-Martin» (Saint-Martin island), which has been completely renewed in a modern, sober style which harmonies perfectly with the modern atmosphere of the Beaubourg. It has maintained its commercial vocation, some galleries have also been reconstructed.

This quarter, now reserved for pedestrians owes its name to the enormous automatic chiming clock (20 m high) called «Le Défenseur du Temps» (the defender of time) by Jacques Monestier. Man must confront the demons from the air (the bird), the sea (the crab) and from the earth (the dragon).

FONTAINE DES INNOCENTS

The square which surrounds the fountain «of the Innocents» is at the centre of the roads reserved for pedestrians and is known as being one of the most beautiful in Paris: it is a much frequented place for walks, above all to go from the Georges Pompidou Centre to the «Forum des Halles».

The steps which lightly raise the square often attract small groups of people, or are used as a podium by «chansonnier», musicians or mimers, who find their occasional audience in the people sitting at the surrounding open air

cafés.

Nowadays it is difficult to imagine that once on this site was a church with its cemetery.

However the renaissance masterpiece, the fountain «des Innocents» by Jean Goujourn is constructed exactly against a corner of that church. The nymphs which are represented there, suggest of their own accord the idea of water, with their light and fluid veils; water which was rare at that time in Paris, and which ran from the vases of the nymphs.

In 1786, the destination of the cemetery to another use and the demolition of the church obliged Pajou to construct the fourth side, which he tried to make identical to the others. This was also covered by a dome.

Only half way through the 19th century did it become a real fountain composed of a central basin with a pedistal.

The bass-reliefs which decorated it are at the Louvre, to prevent their deterioration.

The Fountain des Innocents.

A restaurant in the quarter of the Halles.

The old Halles in a painting by Myr Beeh.

LES HALLES

The present quarter has tried to integrate itself with its surrounding ambient. It was built underground an one side while, on the other it opens into a park and did not want to be too imposing with a gigantic monument (like the Georges Pompidou Centre).

Although it has changed and has become the «Marché de la Mode» (The Fashion Market) it has kept its vocation for merchandise which it has had since the 14th century and has been able to conserve an animation comparable to that of long ago.

In fact, at the beginning of the 12th century it became one of the first Parisian markets, the «Marché des Champeaux», created by Louis VI Le Gros on the cultivated ex marshes.

Philippe Auguste, who wanted to promote the prosperity of Paris, had two buildings constructed for drapers and weavers which were called «Les Halles» (a name which derives from the ancient french word «halla» which means «covered place»). It became a great centre for the exchange of the most varied merchandise, a meeting place and a very lively quarter.

In the 17th century, the surroundings took on a new appearance with the construction of the façade of the church of Saint-Eustache and that of «Halle aux Blés» (corn-exchange market); this forced Louis-Philippe to renew the quarter which had become unhealthy.

Baltard was chosen to construct a pavilion. The other, made of stone, ugly and inconvenient, was demolished to make room for a Halles in metal, inspired by the new station, according to the wishes of Napoleon III.

In this way the famous pavilion of cast iron and glass was born, a synthesis of unity and lightness, which were to become the «Womb of Paris» until the sixties.

A decree in 1962 had les Halles moved towards Rungis in order to free the centre of Paris from the every morning hubbub. Baltard's pavilions were therefore demolished in September 1971 (only one remains, which was then rebuilt at Nogent sur Marne), freeing an area of 30 hectares which will begin a great urban re-arrangement in the centre of Paris.

The old Halles.

The Forum des Halles.

The gardens of the Halles.

THE «FORUM DES HALLES»

This was the first building of the Halles complex and was inaugurated in 1979. It was mainly built in prevision of the creation of an enormous road, underground, and railway network (RER).

At the centre of this square underground complex is a square decorated with the «Pigmalione», a sculpture by Julio Silva; from here there is an imposing oblique staircase in white marble.

The four floors are arranged in a way to capture the maximum of natural light through the large arched windows, which have become characteristic of the «Forum», they seem to wink their eye at the arches of the church of Saint-Eustache.

In this underground city you can find squares, roads which sometimes bring back the past in their names, and they are decorated with ceramics, one of which a «trompe-l'oeil» by Fabio Rieti, the Bestiary by Cueco and the ceiling painted by Attila.

The «Forum» represents an ambiguous interweaving of amusement and spending: it includes more than 200 shops which are as unusual as they are luxurious in all fields, but also numerous cinemas and two museums (the «Musée Grévin II» and the Holography Museum).

JARDIN DES HALLE

A green bridge between the past and the present day, the park of the Halles, completed recently, was planned by L. Arretche with a completely classical conception.

An avenue lined with trees and flower beds connects the fountain «des Innocents» to an amphiteatre square situated at the base of the transept of the church of Saint-Eustache, which, in this way, keeps its perspective.

This park is over a lively underground area, which gives no suspicion of its presence on the surface, where you can discover a universe in which underground architecture is expressed with a certain nobility.

The enormous dimensions (15 m high in place Carrée) bordered by the park have been used to advantage by an architecture which uses different materials and which takes inspiration from capitals, arches and columns.

This part, connected to the Forum, includes essentially public installations: an olympic swimming pool, an «omnisport» hall and an auditorium. An immense glass greenhouse contains rare varieties of plants.

The Forum and the gardens of the Halles.

The gardens and the Forum des Halles.

The Forum and the church of Saint-Eustache.

ÉGLISE SAINT-EUSTACHE

In the 16th century, when the quarter was enlivened by a flourishing merchant activity, which attracted an ever growing crowd, the decision was made to substitute the chapel of Sainte-Agnès (13rd century).

Work for the construction of the present church started in 1532, the model was Notre-Dame de Paris. The construction, with various interruptions, was finished a century later (1640).

The length of time taken to complete the work explains the external shining gothic style and the renaissance decoration inside.

Only the southern façade, which has not been completed, was constructed by Jean Hardouin-Mansart de Jouy in a more classical style.

In 1844 a fire made restauration work necessary and this was carried out by Baltard.

The main façade rises in front of the new Halles park. It is divided into five trellises which are separated by groups of two columns; the balustrades underline three withdrawn floors.

The façade of the transept, flanked by two small towers of stairs which end in skylights are worthy of notice, although they are not very prominent. Its curved doorways have been restaured in the gothic style.

The Virgin's chapel, of a rounded shape, covered by a bell tower, has been hidden by a sacristy, in its lower part, in the 18th century.

Entering the church you will be impressed by the majestic width of the nave, filled with light in a way that gives the impression of lightness.

The complex respects a constant unity of slender pillars, up to the splendor of the vault in blazing style, with ribbing rich with keystones falling in crowns, above all in the choir and in the transept. The mullioned window has arches in its centre separated by pillars.

The generosity of the merchants' confraternity to this church has made it possible for it to gather various works of art. The first amongst these, for example, is the tomb of Colbert.

The statues of fidelity and of Colbert (who is wearing the mantle of the Knights of the Holy Ghost) were sculptured by Coysevox, that of prosperity by Tuby. They were all designed by Le Brun.

The murals of the chapels are from Simon Vouet's workshop. Among other paintings there is «Les disciples d'Emmaüs» (the disciples of Emmaus), a work of Rubens in his youth, a «Tobie et l'ange» (Tobias and the angel) of the Florentine school.

In the chapel of the Virgin, there is a magnificent statue of the Virgin sculptured by Pigalle.

The church of Saint-Eustache still has an important part today in the field of concerts of church music due to its magnificent organ.

The church of Saint-Eustache.

Folklore at Montmartre (fête des Vendanges).

THE BUTTE:
QUARTIER MONTMARTRE

Montmartre, where a Roman temple was built and where only a bronze head of Mercury was found, was, perhaps, dedicated to Mars. However the origin of the name «Mons Martyrum» is due to the christian tradition of the 9th century. It comes from the legend which relates that bishop Saint-Denis, the first evangelizer in Gaul, was beheaded there with his companions Rustique and Eleuthère.

In this way the «Martyrium» was built but the only thing that remains of it is its memory and where it stood which is now occupied by the church of Saint-Pierre-de-Montmartre.

During the Middle Ages Louis VI Le Gros founded the abbey of the Benedectine nuns; and they reigned over the «butte» (hill); nothing remains of the convent buildings. Only the chapel, the church of Saint-Pierre, is still standing thanks to restauration work carried out in various periods.

During the revolution the convent buildings were razed to the ground.

The slopes of the «Butte» were then gashed by chalk caves, which were used in the 19th century for the buildings of Paris. However the caves had to be closed because they threatened the stability of the hill. This, without doubt, is one of the causes of its isolation, even if the Parisians love its countryside atmosphere, with windmills and vineyards on its steep slopes.

After the closure of the caves, houses were built, such as the «Château des brouillards» where Gérard de Nerval lived and the small «guinguettes» (popular open air cafés where you can dance).

In 1871, General Lecomte tried to take over the cannons which had been used for defence against the Prussians. This caused a revolt and General Lecomte was shot. Therefore the Town Hall was born on the Butte Montmartre.

The Sacré-Coeur is the sign of the expiation of the crimes which were committed there.

The «Bateau Lavoir» gave hospitality to the greatest, and at that time poor artists: Renoir, Van Dongen, Modigliani, Picasso, Apollinaire... As far as Toulouse-Lautrec is concerned, he was most often to be seen at the «Moulin Rouge» or at the «Chat Noir».

Today Montmartre is living in the shadow of its past and is trying to prolong the tradition of cabarets, artists and «chansonniers».

How is this zone delimited exactly? Only the ex village of the Butte? Or, as many people think, also by Pigalle, Place Blanche, Clichy?

The inhabitants of the Butte feel independent from those of the «bas». Therefore we have one Montmartre «du haut» (higher) and another «du bas» (lower).

View of Sacré-Coeur.

Characteristic street of Montmartre.

The Moulin Rouge in the day time.

The Moulin Rouge and its romantic effects of nocturnal light.

Place Pigalle.

MONTMARTRE «DU BAS». A nocturnal universe where flashing lighted signs show the cabarets or night clubs overflowing with a multicoloured crowd who animate the quarter in a ferment unknown by day.

Place de Clichy, at one end of the avenue of the same name which was a boundry between the Montmartre and the Batignolles communes, is in a breach in the ex town walls of the «Fermiers Généraux».

The monument to marshal Moncey, which commemorates a battle against the Prussians in 1814, occupies the centre of one of the most important cross roads in Paris.

The avenue de Clichy, surrounded by cinemas, shops and cabarets which are still famous today (the «Cabaret des deux ânes»), leads us to place Blanche (the White Square). Its name was derived from its esplanade which in the past was an obligatory passage for carts full of chalk or flour. The place Blanche is famous above all for the «**Moulin Rouge**», the paradise of the «French Cancan», where the throng crowds to see this typically Parisian performance. It was preceded by a romantic ball room, «La Dame Blanche», then by a revolutionary group at the time of the revolution.

In the entrance hall of this building it is possible to admire the paintings by Toulouse-Lautrec who loved this place.

MONTMARTRE «DU HAUT». This corresponds to the «butte». It is probably for this

Pictures of the French dance «cancan», painted by Toulouse-Lautrec.

Sacré-Coeur at night.

Sacré-Coeur: the interior.

On the right page a complete view of the basilica of the Sacré-Coeur.

Sacré-Coeur: the funicolar-railway.

reason that the natives of Paris consider it the only authentic Montmartre. The «butte» still has its own particular fascination today. It has kept its slightly rustic style in its narrow roads and its steep stairways with central handrails.

It is necessary to climb to the top. The most courageous can climb the steps of the monumental stairway (end of the 19th century) which lead to the Sacré-Coeur. Others can take the funicular.

BASILIQUE DU SACRÉ-COEUR

This is an enormous white mass outlined against the sky of Paris, it is a centre of attraction and at the same time it is almost more of an attraction than the historical monuments of the capital, in spite of the fact that the aesthetics is relative. However it must not be forgotten that this church is a place of pilgrimage and is not a parish church.

Its building was decided by the National Assembly in 1873 according to the wishes of the catholics, as pennance for the crimes perpetrated by the Commune. Money for the erection of this gigantic monument was obtained with appropriation of funds by the government, and by public offerings and subscriptions. The project of romanesque-bizantine style by Paul Abadie was approved. Work was started in 1875 and was finished in 1910; the church was only consecrated in 1919.

As the land is friable due to the caves, it was necessary to excavate wells for the foundations with a depth of 38 m to support the building.

The basilica is surmounted by an ovoid dome with skylights and four minor domes. The bell tower, 84 metres high, was constructed and connected to the basilica of Lucien Magne in 1910. The bell tower contains the famous «Savoyarde», a bell weighing about 18 tons, given by the Savoy diocese, which needed 28 horses for transport.

The interior is mainly decorated with mosaics. Olivier Merson represented the devotion of France to the Sacred Heart with an immense mosaic of 500 square metres.

The cript, which is much more sober in style, contains religious works of art of the age. From the top of the dome you can enjoy a marvellous view for a range of 50 km.

The «Vie de Bohème».

Place du Tertre.

Rue Nervin. On the right a palette in Place du Tertre.

PLACE DU THÉÂTRE

This was the village square; here the gallows of the «Dames de Montmartre» and the king stood.

At the end of the 1870 many cannons were gathered in this square, those which general

The Cabaret «Lapin Agile»: detail of the façade.

On the right: the Vineyard.

The Lapin Agile and, below, the Moulin de la Galette.

Lecomte tried to seize provoking a revolt which gave origin to the Commune.

Now it has become the lively nightime centre of the «butte» Montmartre, where artists paint in the square as their predecessors did, and the night clubs all around give it a colourful note.

However it is still possible to savour its true rustic nature early in the morning, when it is deserted: it seems like a different scene, made of small houses, and one can be lost in the fascination it gives out.

THE VIGNE

This is the last vineyard of the «butte» on the corner between rue Saint-Vincent and rue des Saules; it reminds us of the importance which the monarchs gave to these plantations, which reached the Marais.

Every year the vine-harvest festival (con-

ceived by Pierre Labric in 1920) gives place to a picturesque procession and to sale by auction of cases, decorated by a local painter, of the must pressed in the Mairie cellars, for the benefit of the old inhabitants of Montmartre.

«LE LAPIN AGILE»

The small house at the foot of the vineyard has kept its appearance of long ago.

In 1860 it was a «guinguette» with the pompous name of «au rendez-vous des», which became the «cabaret des assassins».

In 1860 it was a «guinguette» with the pompous name of «au rendez-vous des voleurs», which became the «cabaret des assassins».
owes its name to the painting, called «le lapin à Gill» (Gill's rabbit), while it is still a popular concert café called «Ma compagnarde».

The owner, Frédéric Gérard, gave it the definite name of «le lapin agile» (the agile rabbit) in 1903. Later it was Aristide Bruant to make sure of its survival.

This cabaret, frequented by many penniless artists, such as Apollinaire, Max Jacob, Picasso, Vläminck... and by men of the world, had an important role in the artistic life of Montmartre.

MOULIN DE LA GALETTE

Immortalized in a painting by Renoir and others by many other artists, it was a famous popular dance hall in the 19th century. The idea of this kind of premises was of the son of the Debray millers who were massacred by the Prussians. Nicolas Charles Debray, the only survivor, found himself to be the owner of two mills: the «Blute fin» and the «Radet».

Initially he transformed the «Radet», which he called «Moulin de la Galette». Then there were changes and the name passed to the «Blute fin», which has it still today.

From a dance hall it became a variety theatre and then a studio for radio and television transmissions, and lastly it became an ORTF studio.

The «Radet» is only a copy of 1925 and is in front of the entrance to the Théâtre du Tertre.

Place des Vosges: pavillon de la Reine.

THE MARAIS

The marais was once a marshy area where an arm of the Seine flowed into. During the 12th century the military order of Jerusalem's Temple established there a priorship and some agricultural estates. Later other religious congregations settled along the edges of the Roman road leading to Melun (now rue Saint-Antoine).

But this quarter became Parisian only at the end of the 14th century, when it was incorporated in Charles V's boundary walls; in this period the king leaves the palace of the Cité to establish at the hotel Saint-Paul, between the Seine and rue Saint-Antoine. There in 1393 the famous «bal des ardents» took place where some friends of Charles VI, dressed up as savages, burnt like torches.

Of this hotel, demolished under Francis I, only street names remain, such as rue de Beautrillis, rue de la Cerisaie, rue des jardins Saint-Paul. In front of this hotel was that of des Tournelles, purchased by Charles VI (in 1407). There Henry II died, after the tournament in which Montgomery pierced a spear through one of his eyes (in 1559). Caterina de Medici, mad with grief, left the hotel and obtained that her son Charles IX razed it to the ground.

The 17th century is the golden age of the marais. Henry IV had been the author of the deep transformations of the quarter which would be completed under the kings Louis XIII and Louis XIV. He was the first of the town-planner kings, and it has been written that «as soon as he was master of Paris only masons at work could be seen». He had made a grand project of urbanization which included a «place de France» where 8 streets should come out, denominated after names of French provinces. The names «rue de Bretagne», «rue de Saintonge», «rue de Beauce», and so on, evoke today this never realized project. In return, the king's project of building a royal square which could serve to the inhabitants of the city as a sheltered place for walking, would be carried out since 1605. The square became rapidly a fashionable meeting-place, aristocratic and popular at the same time. Noblemen, high officials and rich private citizens had their habitations built around it, between courtyard and garden, destined to become the ideal model of the private hôtel common in 18th-century Europe.

The religious role of the quarter had too a great impulse, especially because the Jesuits settled in rue Saint-Antoine. Literary life reigns in the numerous drawing-rooms: the one of the marquioness de Sévigné, rue de la Culture Sainte-Cathérine, the precious drawing-room of M.lle de Scudéry, rue de Beauce, the hôtel d'Angoulême where Boileau, Racine, père Bourdaloue, M.me de Sévigné, Régnard meet. In 1634 the «théatre du Marais» is established, where the famous actors of the Marais, direct ancestors of French actors, perform for the first time the Cid by Corneille. Music too was present, with the ballets and the sarabands that were danced at Sully's, or the concerts of sacred music given at Saint-Paul's by the chapel-master Marc-Antoine Charpentier and by the organist Richard Delalande.

The 18th century shifts fashion towards Saint-Louis Island, and above all towards the west. Some wonderful buildings however date back to this century, such as the hôtel de Soubise and the hôtel de Rohan. But commerce, craftsmanship and later industry invaded the quarter; this phenomenon precipitated during the revolution, when hotels and monasteries were declared national property. Only since 1962, date of the Malraux law, a complete recovery of the entire area can be carried out.

Place des Vosges: statue of Louis XIII, detail.

PLACE DES VOSGES

King Henry IV has here magnificently developed his building activity. In France, no other square — apart from place Vendôme, more recent — is so wide and harmonious at the same time. The king's lands, divided into small parts were sold to private citizens. Planning a square arranged in a uniform way, the royal contract of 1605 stated precisely that the building should be in stone and bricks with slate roofs

Pavillon du Roi: Henry IV.

Place des Vosges.

Café and arcade in Place des Vosges.

It also prescribed the opening of shops under the arcades which ran along the whole perimeter of the square. The project was successfully realized. The 36 palaces were inhabited by high society and the use of freestone and bricks, harmoniously combined, became a characteristic of the architecture under Louis XIII.

The young Louis XIII and Anne of Austria unveiled the square celebrating their engagement with a grandiose «carousel of the knights of glory» which lasted 4 days (April 1612). The royal square became then the centre of elegant life in Paris. M.me de Sévigné was born there

(at n. 1 bis), there Bossuet (at n. 17), Richelieu (at n. 21), Marion de l'Orme lived, there competitions, tournaments and rides took place. The **equestrian statue of Louis XIII** was placed there by Richelieu in 1639 (but the present monument is a reproduction of the 19th century).

At the end of the 18th century the square becomes out-of-date and assumes a provincial look. The Consulate names it after the department (Vosges) which is the first to pay taxes. Victor Hugo lived at n. 6, today a museum with original drawings of the poet, the complete collection of the editions of his works and a library of critical works.

PAVILLON DU ROI

On the axis of rue de Birague (formerly rue royale), the king's palace rises on high arcades. It constituted the main entrance of the square, especially on the occasion of processions coming from rue Saint-Antoine. On the façade facing the square is a medallion representing the king's profile, and some «H» surrounded by palms and trophies. On the opposite side is the Queen's palace, similar but simpler.

HÔTEL DE SULLY

This hôtel, one of the wonders of the marais, was built by Jean Androuët du Cerceau in 1624, and purchased ten years later by the ex-minister of Henry IV, Sully, who lived there for seven years. His neighbour M.me de Sévigné often went there on a visit, especially on the day when she looked at Voisin while she was being taken to the stake.

The hôtel is built, according to the by now classical plan, between «courtyard and garden». The portal opens on an arcade which unites two rigorously made small villas. Entering the courtyard one is amazed for the magnificence of the decorations. The façades are adorned with win-

Place des Vosges: detail.

Hôtel de Sully: building and garden.

On the right: Hôtel de Sully.

spective effects with the semicircular apse. On the cross-vault of the transept the dome rises, on pendentives with the four evangelists sculptured in the centre of medallions. Worth noting are a «Christ au jardin des oliviers» by Delacroix and above all the pathetic «Vierge de douleur» by Germain Pilon (1586) in the chapel on the left side of the choir.

dows with cornices and pediments, and dormers full of sculptures. And, above all, the first floor is decorated with bas-reliefs: on the body of the building human figures symbolizing autumn and winter, on the wings the symbols of the «four elements», and finally the other two seasons on the side of the garden.

Sully had a small hôtel built, the «orangerie», in the back part of the garden; for his usual walk the duke went this way as far as place des Vosges.

ÉGLISE SAINT-PAUL-SAINT-LOUIS

Church of Saint-Paul-Saint-Louis seen from rue de Sévigné.

In 1580 the Jesuits settle in rue Saint-Antoine, in their professed house, today Charlemagne Lyceum. In the area of the present church was a chapel dedicated to Saint-Louis. But in 1595 the Jesuits, involved in the Ligue, are forced to leave France. They stand high in the king's favour again since 1606, under Louis XIII, and can build a church worthy of their company. It became a centre of worldly life thanks to its musicians and orators. Father Bourdaloue's preaches were real events, as M.me de Sévigné tells in her letters.

The foundation stone was laid in 1627. The design, conceived by the Jesuit Martellange, drew its inspiration from the Church of Gesù in Rome. The dome, chief innovation of the Jesuitic style, is awkwardly erected, in that it is partly hidden by the façade. The sculptural decoration becomes richer the more the building rises. On the top the coat-of-arms of France and Navarre are represented.

Inside: the wide nave, full of light, is flanked by round arches which lead into the chapels. The latter, according to Baroque taste, are communicating and in this way produce lively per-

RUE FRANÇOIS MIRON

A part of the former rue Saint-Antoine, it is named after a provost of the merchants under Henry IV.

It starts magnificently with the **Church Saint-Gervais-Saint-Protais,** one of the oldest parish churches of the right bank (6th century). The 17th-century Jesuitic façade is applied on a late-Gothic building (15th-16th century).

The buildings from n. 2 to n. 14 form a remarkable whole of the early 18th century, picturesquely flanked to the church. At n. 2 and 4 the Couperins lived, outstanding composers and organists of Saint-Gervais's.

At n. 13, some **columbary-like houses** of the 15th century evoke Paris under Louis XI. N. 68, **hôtel de Beauvais.** M.me de Beauvais was maid and confidante of queen Anne of Austria; she, who first put young Louis XIV wise (in 1654), succeeded with some intrigues in having a hôtel built in rue Saint-Antoine by Lepeautre, architect of the king.

The space being limited, the architect could not adopt the classical arrangement «between courtyard and garden»; he then chose to build the main façade onto the street. The portico is formed by a fine roundish peristyle, facing a perfectly proportioned oval courtyard.

HÔTEL DE SENS

The diocese of Paris was supported by the archbishops of Sens until 1623; often cardinals they were of so great importance in managing the affairs of the reign that they often had to reside in Paris. One of them, Tristan de Salazar, man of letters and fond of art, had one of the finest habitations in Paris built: the hôtel de Sens. Built between 1474 and 1519, it is in the

Hôtel de Sens.

flamboyant Gothic style, and is one of the rare extant monuments of the Middle Ages in Paris. It has an unusual look, being a fortress — for the corner small towers and the imposing built-in tower — and at the same time sumptuous habitation for the elegance of the portico and the dormers adorned with coat-of-arms and pinnacles.

Tristan's successors did not all inhabit the hôtel. Under the Ligue the hôtel served as «headquarters». Then Henry IV gave it as a gift to his former wife, queen Margot, who led there a gallant life. But she soon felt a strong aversion for the hôtel: one of her favourites was killed under the portal by a jealous rival, who was later beheaded in the same place at the queen's request; she watched the execution from the window on the right side of the door. From 1622 until the revolution the hôtel was rented to noble chevaliers, then to a coach enterprise.

Since 1961, it has housed the Forney library.

RUE DE FRANCS BOURGEOIS

This very ancient street owes its name to the «maisons d'aumônes» destined since the 14th century to the poor, called «francs bourgeois» because they were exempted from some taxes.

Hôtel Carnavalet (entrance at n. 23 of rue de Sévigné). Architectural masterpiece and historical museum of Paris, the hôtel Carnavalet is of remarkable interest. A Renaissance habitation and a 17th-century one are harmoniously interlaced. The marquioness of Sévigné left here the major trace. In love with the marais where she had been born, she rented the hôtel from 1677 until her death in 1696. She received visitors in her famous drawing-room and wrote there many of her letters. In the 17th century the hôtel was inhabited by magistrates and businessmen, then the Restoration destined it to the École des Ponts et Chaussées.

Hôtel Carnavalet: internal yard and details.

The hôtel Carnavalet is originally an early-Renaissance habitation, the only example in Paris of the private architecture of that epoch (apart from the hôtel de Scipion Sardini, located in rue Scipion at n. 13). Built in 1548, and traditionally ascribed to the architect Pierre Lescot, this was one of the first hôtels designed between courtyard and garden. In the following century, remarkable alterations were made under the direction of François Mansart (uncle of the architect of Louis XIV); the two side wings and the façade onto rue de Sévigné were increased by one floor, giving the hôtel its present look.

Onto the street the façade is relatively simple. The ashlar-worked portico is adorned with sculptures by Jean Goujon (16th century): in the keystone, a personification of Plenty, in the pediment a great quantity of trophies surrounds a medallion. The main body faces the courtyard of honour, with the two adjacent palaces and the two wings. Some undeniably Italian characteristics contribute to the success of the whole, such as the balustrade and, above all, the space left to the carved ornaments. Four big isolated figures representing the seasons alternate with the windows of the piano nobile: they are a work of Jean Goujon and form a precious group of Renaissance French school. In the centre of the courtyard is the bronze statue of Louis XIV, a work by Coysevox. The only royal statue escaped from the systematic destruction of the revolutionaries initially adorned the large courtyard of the Hôtel de Ville.

Around the former garden parts of buildings of the 16th, 17th and 18th century have been added in 1889, transported from different zones of Paris and linked the one to the other by passageways; they are the Arc de Nazareth, which stepped over an alley near the Palais de Justice, and is ornamented with sculptures by Jean Goujon; the façade of the hôtel de Choiseul and the one of the Palais des Drapiers. Finally, the 20th

Hôtel Salé, seat of the Picasso Museum.

Nude lying down

Dora Naar

of the hôtel Clisson (14th century), whose only trace is a fortified door. As soon as François de Rohan, prince of Soubise, purchased the hôtel in 1700, he had it transformed by the architect Delamaire.

The main body, recessed in comparison with the rest of the building, is emphasized by this characteristic, made possible by a wide court yard surrounded by a fine colonnade. But the courtyard had also another function: to serve as a riding-ground for the royal company of gen darmes whose colonel was François de Rohan. The façade, of classical style, is adorned with superb statues by Robert le Lorrain represent ing the four seasons. The triangular pediment is surmounted by «la gloire», «la magnificence» and by four groups of children, sculptured by the same artist. The apartments, whose deco ration was ordered to Germain Boffrand, con sist particularly of the two oval halls, master pieces of the French rocaille style.

The Soubise palace communicates with the hôtel de Rohan Soubise, this too a work of the architect Delamaire.

HÔTEL SALÉ

Or hôtel Aubert de Fontenay (5, rue de Thorigny). In 1656 the undertaker of the «Gabelles», Pierre Aubert de Fontenay, had a hôtel built by Jean Boullier; the profits he made out of the tax on salt won to his habitation the popular nickname of «hôtel Salé».

The courtyard of honour, semicircular, pre cedes the main body. The beautiful façade, with

century has enlarged the museum with modern constructions.

The rich collections recall the history of Paris since Francis I with paintings, insignia, relief schemes, etc. Moreover, wood coverings of Parisian hôtels were brought back here, and transformed the halls in shrines of furniture.
The hôtel de Lamoignon (entrance from rue Pavée) is a finest example of mid-16th-century architecture. Today it is the seat of the histori cal library of the city of Paris.
Hôtel de Soubise (at n. 60 of rue des Francs Bourgeois). This building was built in the area

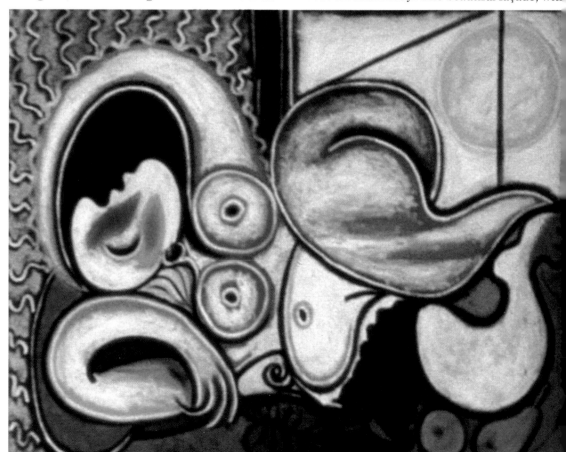

Flute of Pan
Woman and Child
Show hall
Head of woman

the two pediments animated by female divinities, children, dogs and rich garlands of flowers, is surmounted on the side of the garden by a sculptured pediment and by garrets «à la Mansart».

In the 19th century the hôtel was destined to commercial activities which disfigured it. Fortunately, the monumental great staircase after the Roman fashion, richly sculptured, was not modified. The city of Paris has recently undertaken the restoration of the hôtel and of the garden. The interior has been arranged so that it can house the Picasso Museum, open to the public since 28th September 1985. The collections here contained are precious: in addition to numerous works by Picasso (who died in 1973) there are paintings lovingly purchased by him during his almost 100-year-long life. The designers of the museum (the architect Roland Simounet and the curator Dominique Bozo) have been able to create a harmony between the most baroque among Parisian hôtels and the most provocative and deeply-rooted in modernity among the artists of the 20th century.

THE «GRANDS BOULEVARDS»

Rue de l'Opéra.

These are long avenues which follow the line of the ancient walls of Paris for a length of 4.5 km.

The fortifications, which were in a very bad state, were demolished under Louis XIV, when peace seemed to reign in France. The moats were filled and became tree lined avenues, flanked by gardens, private hôtels and convents.

The boulevards were really created in the 18th century, but they did not reach their maximum glory until the following century. They then became one of the main centres of Parisian life, boasting literature, politics, publications, theatre, fashion. There, the most important «café restaurants» of the time rose (Café Tortoni, Café Riche, Café Divan, Café Napol tain).

The boulevard des Italiens, ex boulevard d Gand under the Restoration, saw all the lates fashions of the time go by: the Muscadins an the Merveilleuses under the Directory, then th Gandins and later the Dandys and the Lions. To day it has become a business centre, as the im posing façades of the banks testify.

Having gone past the carrefour (cross road: Richelieu-Drouot the atmosphere slowl changes and the Montmartre, Poissonière, D Bonne Nouvelle, Saint-Denis and Saint-Marti boulevards become increasingly popular as yo get nearer to the place de la République.

Grevin Museum.

Shopping centre.

There you can find multicoloured shop win dows, large cafés with small tables in the ope on the wide pavements, a large number of cin mas, of well known theatres («Théâtre de variétés», «Le Gymnase»,...) and small ga leries which bring past centuries to mind.

The Grévin Museum which is attractive bu a little disquieting — in Montmartre boulevard - was created in 1882 by the caricaturist Grévi a fantastic museum with dim lights containin wax works representig famous people and building dedicated to prestidigitation. Ever thing there is magical and enchanting.

Towards the west, two triumphal arches hav been erected, in honour of Louis XIV: the «**port** **Saint-Martin**», built in 1674, celebrates the vi tories of Louis XIVth over the German, Dutc and Spanish armies; the other arch, built in 167: the «**porte Saint-Denis**», is also in memory c

Boulevard des Italiens.

Porte Saint Denis. Below: Porte Saint Martin and a detail of the monument in Place de la République.

the victories of Louis XIV in Germany.

Place de la République, at a crossroads of the Grands Boulevards, was organized by Haussmann in 1854.

The monument of the République by Morice was only placed there in 1883 in the place of the ramparts of the ex «porte du Temple».

Besides this square, the Grands Boulevards continue with the boulevards du Temple des Filles du Calvaire and with boulevard de Beaumarchais until they reach the Bastille. These avenues have become a historical route for processions and demonstrations, especially on the 1st May.

The columns of Place de la Nation.

On the left: the monument of Place de la République.

Place de la Bastille: detail of the Columns of July (1840).

PLACE DE LA NATION

Once this square was called place du Trône, because an immense throne had been erected there for Louis XIV and his wife, the Infanta Marie Thérèse. The throne was destroyed during the Revolution and the Convention installed one of the guillotines of Paris there and called the square place du Trône versé (Square of the upturned throne). Napoleon had dreamed of a perspective which connected place de la Nation and place de la Bastille to the Louvre but only the starting point of this perspective, the Arc de Triomphe, was built. The present name was given in 1880 for the first celebration of the anniversary of the 14th July.

At the centre of the square, in a small garden, is a basin decorated with a bronze group sculptured by Dalou with the figure of the Triomphe de la République, which was originally intended for place de la République.

The square is the starting point of avenue du Trône, framed by two columns surmounted by statues of Philippe Auguste and of Saint-Louis and is lengthened by cours de Vincennes.

A few years ago the «Foire du Trône» (fair of the Throne) was held there, it was also called «Foire au pain d'épice» (the gingerbread fair) which, due to the disturbance it caused to the surrounding inhabitants, was moved to the Bois de Vincennes on the field of Reuilly near the Daumesnil lake.

PLACE DE LA BASTILLE

The Bastille, built between 1370 and 1382, was originally a fortress before it became a prison. Among the famous prisoners, there were the mysterious Masque de Fer (The Man in the Iron Mask), the lord of Bassompierre, Mirabeau and the turbulent Chevalier Latude who stayed there for 28 years and escaped 3 times.

In 1789 the Paris mob siezed this citadel and the day was soon saluted as marking the triumph of popular insurrection over the arbitrary power of the crown (the king's order was sufficient to be imprisoned). 83 models of the citadel were sculptured in its own stones and were sent to the provinces in memory of royal despotism. Two of these models are kept at the Carnavalet museum.

The confines of the ex fortress are still indicated by a line of coloured cubes.

Today in the centre of the square is the «colonne de Juillet» (the July Column) in

Place de la Bastille: The Columns of July (1840), 47 metres high, overlooked by the Genious of Liberty.

memory of the revolution of July 1830.

Under the column a marble base contains the tomb of the victims of these battles; their names are engraved on the bronze shaft of the column.

From the height of its 47 metres, the numen of liberty towers over the square. It is possible to climb to the top up a staircase of 238 steps, there is a beautiful view of the mount Sainte-Geneviève and the Marais quarter.

The Bastille quarter is the meeting point of two different worlds: on one side is the historical city organized urbanistically (rue Saint-Antoine, boulevard Morland) with the new boulevards and parks of the Second Empire (boulevard Beaumarchais and Richard Lenoir); on the other side are the ancient suburbs which conserve the more ancient traces of the Parisian village.

The creation of an «Opéra Populaire» is included in a transformation programme of the quarter, respecting its tradition. The novelty of place de la Bastille consists in the architectural and human variety of which it is formed.

The Canadian architect Carlos Ott won an international competition for the construction of the new Opéra.

The work is being rapidly carried out; the ex station of Vincennes, the Paramount cinema and some arches in rue de Lyon and avenue Daumesnil have been demolished.

In March 1982, the President of the Republic F. Mitterrand made the decision of supplying the capital with an «Opéra Populaire» which is modern, commodious and profitable.

A large hall of 2700 places is forseen, with 5 spaces to be kept free in order to allow a quick alternation of spectacles, a hall of 1500 places which can be modulated, the «maison de l'Opéra», a laboratory for creating and storing scenary. In all this covers an area of 90,000 mq.

The present Minister of Culture (F. Léotard) has tried to combine the initial project with the requirements of the capital.

The Opéra de la Bastille is changing into a simple auditorium, leaving all its prestige and activity to the Garnier Palace.

Monument to Frédéric Chopin.

On the right: «le Petit Temple» in Parc des Buttes Chaumont.

CIMETIÈRE DU PÈRE LACHAISE

This is the biggest and most visited cemetery in Paris, measuring 45 hectares. The slightly hilly land gives the impression of being in a garden and there is nothing gloomy about going for a stroll there. Numerous celebrities are burried there, among whom we can mention: **Apollinaire, Nerval, Molière, Sarah Bernhardt, Musset, Chopin, Balzac, La Fontaine, Modigliani, Géricault, Ingres, Lavoisier, Raspail, Edith Piaf, Simone Signoret, Allan Kardec,** founder of the spiritualist philosophy whose tomb is the most flowery.

Once it was the rest home of the Jesuits, in fact its name is that of Father Lachaise, confessor of Louis XIV.

In 1763 the Jesuits were expelled and the property was taken over by the town. In 1803 Napoleon gave orders for Brongniart to transform the land into a cemetery.

In the north eastern corner is the «mur des Fédérés» (the wall of the Federates) where the 147 defenders of the Commune who had taken refuge in the cemetery were shot by the inhabitants of Versailles.

The columbarium beside the Muslim cemetery is noteworthy and decorated with a sculpture by Paul Landowski in its cellar.

PARC DES BUTTES CHAUMONT

At the top of Belleville is one of the most romantic and also the most surprising parks in Paris: the Buttes Chaumont park.

It was simple undefined land, haunted by thieves and the like, where there were quarries and windmills. In 1864 Napoleon III had it made into a park by Haussmann. He made it into an unusual park in English style, with hills, woods, hidden grottos, disconnected rocks and paths dotted with kiosks.

The lake is surprising, with an island in the centre made of rocks 50 m high reached either by a bridge built in bricks, called «of the suicides» or by a small wooden footbridge. All is dominated by a small temple inspired by the temple of the Sibyl at Tivoli, from where it is possible to admire Montmartre and Saint-Denis.

BOIS DE VINCENNES

This is a great open space of green to the east of Paris in correspondance to the Bois de Boulogne, it is the «Green Lung» of the capital and is the largest park of the city with its 929 hectares.

It was already royal hunting land and covered the immense woodland region called Lanchonia Silva which stretched past the Marne.

Philippe Auguste had a fence of 12 km built, to keep in stags and deer. In the 13th century Charles V had the Château de Beauté built at Nogent. As from the 18th century, the woods became much appreciated by numerous Parisians who went there and the forest was planted with new trees. Unfortunately it was devastated by the revolutionary troops.

In 1860, Napoleon III gave the wood to the City in order to have it transformed into an English style public park. Haussmann was entrusted with the work, and created, among the trees and the avenues, the lakes of Saint-Mandé, Daumesnil and des Minimes (the last name derives from the religious order of the Minim friars who had been given the area of the lake by Louis VII); and a race course was also created.

Bois de Vincennes: children playing.

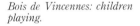

THE CHÂTEAU DE VINCENNES

Lac Daumesnil (Château de Vincennes).

Saint-Louis, who had always been attracted by Bois de Vincennes, decided to have the Saint-Chapelle erected there; the image of Saint-Louis administering justice under his oak tree is a well known image. At the same time as the chapel, the construction of the famous Vincennes stronghold was started.

The imposing square keep is 52 m tall, flanked by four turrets at the corners and surrounded by mighty walls strengthened by wide moats and high towers. It is a true fortress. It was started during the reign of Philippe VI and was only finished in 1370 to give hospitality to princes every so often.

In the 17th century, Mazarino, governor of Vincennes, asked the architect Le Vau to add some living quarters: the King's pavilion and the Queen's Pavilion.

A century later the keep became a state prison where some famous people, such as Diderot, who escaped various times, Prince de Conti, the marquis de Sade, the Duke d'Enghien who was shot in the moat, were imprisoned.

Under Louis-Philippe, Vincennes became, like the Bastille, a fortress for the defence of Paris and was fortified by casemates.

It was necessary to wait for the first restoration work carried out by Viollet le Duc at the request of Napoleon III, to rediscover this imposing fortress with its moats.

The existing towers were demolished; only the «Bois» tower, which Le Vau shortened and which became the main entrance and the «Village» tower 42 m high, remain.

The Bois de Vincennes also has a zoological garden and floral park.

The zoological garden, with its famous rock 72 m high, now dominion of moufflons, is one of the last remains of the colonial exhibition which took place in 1931. The hundreds of mammals and birds which can be admired there have made it the most important zoo in France.

Another attraction is the floral park, this is more recent because it was created in 1969 for flower exhibitions; it is an enchantment of colours and beauty.

The 28 hectares of the park include, among multiple varieties of flowers, small pavilions — where, every so often, exhibitions are held — and a play space for children. Vincennes, much appreciated because of its pleasant wood strewn with lakes, is very animated thanks to the zoological garden and the floral park.

Its castle, a fortress with thick walls, makes it a surprising curiosity at the doors of Paris.

The donjon of Château de Vincennes.

An elephant in the park.

BOIS DE BOULOGNE

The Orangerie de Bagatelle.

A reserve of green to the west of Paris, much frequented by the Parisians, the Bois de Boulogne offers its 900 hectares of lawns, woods, lakes and avenues (95 km) to sports enthusiasts, children and passers by.

At the beginning it was a forest of thorns where deer were hunted. It took on its present name when, in the 14th century, the church of Notre-Dame-de-Boulogne-Le-Petit was built. However the Bois de Boulogne, full of bandits and brigands was not a safe place and so Henry II decided to surround it with a wall with eight doors.

A hundred years later the wood, put into order by Colbert, with strait roads and crossroads marked by crosses as in the royal parks, opened its doors at the request of Louis XIV.

In 1815 the Bois was devastated by the Russian and English armies.

In 1852, Napoleon III handed the wood over to the city of Paris and it was rearranged using Hyde Park in London as a model, according to the fashion of the period. In fact the work carried out was a real novelty, the lakes form an immense area of water of 11 hectares — with an island in the centre which can be reached by canoe —, an artificial waterfall, the Pré Catelan and the climatic garden (a park of attractions for children).

The park rapidly attracted the Parisians and

The Château de Bagatelle.

The Trianon de Bagatelle.

became a centre of elegance; restaurants and a Swiss chalet were built.

Horses were also catered for: in the hippodrome of Long-champs important races take place.

In the modern buildings of the Musée National des Arts et Traditions Populaires (National Museum of the Arts and Popular Traditions) numerous objects and documents relative to popular art from its origins to today are displayed.

In the magnificent Bagatelle park is a small castle of the 18th century surrounded by a garden in English style, well known due to its splendid rose gardens.

This complex is the result of a «wager» between Marie Antoniette and her brother-in-law, the Count d'Artois. The future Charles X, who bought the pavilion in ruins from Marshal d'Estrées in 1775, promised to construct a building in less than 3 months, and so he did. This park was handed over to the City of Paris in 1905.

THE VILLETTE

The Villette.

The Villette, situated in a valley between the «Butte de Montmartre» and the «Buttes Chaumont», an enormous area on the outskirts of Paris, is part of the plan of a new urban policy which proposes to re-establish the equilibrium of the capital eastwards.

The Villette is now the object of one of the biggest urban plans of a cultural order which has international resonance.

The basin which has fed the city of Paris with water since 1808 made this district a popular centre.

The first general slaughter houses constructed under Napoleon III, had become very old, and they were modernized in 1955, which was a flourishing period for France, so euphorically it was decided to build the most modern slaughter houses in the world.

In 1974 the «Villette scandal» broke out: work had to be interrupted for economic reasons. As a result these 55 hectares were abandoned until Valéry Giscard d'Estaing, following an idea by Roger Taillibert, took into consideration Adrien Fainsilber's project for a museum and a park in September 1980.

In his turn François Mitterrand backed this project and added a «Cité de la Musique».

Since then the 55 hectares have been dedicated to culture and science, devided into three complexes of vast proportions: *la Cité des Sciences, des Techniques et de l'Industrie, la Cité de la Musique, and le parc*; and in others conceived for the life of the town, the du Zenith concert hall, the Grande Halle, the Présent theatre; and of the district: cinemas, restaurants...

The Villette: the renowned Géode.

The Palais Omnisport in Bercy.

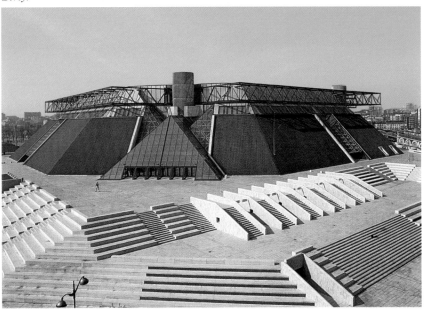

THE BERCY OMNISPORT PALACE

After years of waiting and negotiation and after long months of building, the Omnisport Palace has taken the place of the Bercy ex wine ware houses.

In February 1984 it opened its doors to receive a cyclist race: the 6 days of Paris.

It looks like a ship covered with a lawn left by the Seine, at Bercy, among the secular plane trees which have seen so much water, so much wine and so many controversies go past.

In 1977 the mayor of Paris, Jacques Chirac, decided to create a great Polyvalent sports complex in Paris.

Paris International Centre - Congress Building.

The airport of Roissy-Charles-de-Gaulle.

The airport of Orly West.

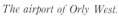

life Parisian

1. *The banks of the Seine and bookstalls.*
2. *Loaf of bread.*
3. *Beggar on a bridge in Paris.*
4. *Underground entrance in modern style.*
5. *Policeman.*

6. *Old streets in Paris.*
7. *Rer station.*
8. *Flower market.*
9. *Children's roundabout in a square.*
10. *Greenhouse.*
11. *Shopping centre.*

life Parisian

1. The «Grand Café».
2. Galeries Lafayette.
3. Folies Bergères theatre.
4. A great jeweler's - Cartier.
5. Cabaret The Lido.
6. Wallace Fountain and Morris Column.
7. A great fashion designer - Christian Dior.
8. A cabaret - the Crazy Horse.
9. Café terrace (La Palette in Montparnasse).
10. Café terrace (Le Fouquet's in the Champs-Elysées).
11. A great restaurant (Laperousse).

BASILIQUE SAINT-DENIS

«Les Gisants» of Saint-Denis.

Basilica of Saint-Denis.

Cathedral since 1966. A legend narrates the foundation of this church: at the beginning of the 5th century, Saint-Denis, the first bishop of Lutetia, evangelist of Gaul, was martyred at Montmartre and then started to walk with his head under his arm. He was buried in the place where he fell and soon after, in 475, a church was built there which became a place of pilgrimage. Besides relics of saints, insignia of royal power such as the oriflamme, the coronation clothes, the Saint-Ampoule were kept there.

From 1140, Abbot Suger, minister to King Louis VII, decided to build a large church and established to project. Its importance in the history of art is enormous: Saint-Denis is the «laboratory» of the gothic style. Its shape is

above all an answer to the new conception of the relationship between God and his creation, a neo-platonic theory elaborated by the Abbot Suger. By this time God was light, even the most vile of things participated in the divine being because it possessed an interior light which came from God. The cathedral is therefore conceived to illuminate man, the light must unify space and the windows must disclose hidden truths.

Description. In the façade, even if it is romantic, there is a characteristic element of the gothic period: the rose window. The narthex is full of pointed arch cross vaults which were still experimental. The nave, of the purest of lines, brought in a grandiose way to the apse, where the great innovation of the basilica can be found: the deambulatorium is united to the chapels by a single system of vaults, in such a way as to give an undulatory effect. Besides this (in the 12th century) P. de Montreuil opened windows in the higher parts of the basilica accentuating the effects of light.

The lying down statues. From the 10th century the basilica became the burial place of the Kings of France and of some great people of the Crown. However the oldest figures go back to the reign of Saint-Louis, who had ordered them for the tombs of his predecessors. This magnificent group of tombs illustrates the evolution of funerary art from Saint-Louis to the Renaissance. It is evident that the 14th century, with for example, the lying figure of Charles V by Beauneveu, introduced the art of the true portrait. With the Renaissance the monumental art of two floor mausoleums was developed. On the lower floor are the royal couple, their rigid, nude bodies are treated with a moving realism. The upper floor shows them on their knees, dressed in ceremonial clothes, their faces serene. The works carried out by Philibert de l'Orme and Pierre Bontemps (the monument of Louis XII and Anne of Brittany and the monuments of Francis I and Claude of France) are superb examples.

The large-windows of the basilica of Saint-Denis.

On the right «les Gisants».

VERSAILLES

Equestrian statue of Louis XIV in the Cour Royale

On the 6th October 1789 the royal family left Versailles for Paris for ever. On the morning of that tragic day the revolutionaries had invaded the castle forcing the Queen to take refuge, as a last resort, with the King. Shortly after, he had to appear on the balcony of the Cour de Marbre in the company of La Fayette, who was then the commander of the National Guard of Paris. The Queen herself notwithstanding the advice of her councillers, had to present herself before the menacing crowd. This courageous action earned her an unhoped for acclamation which could even be heard in the Place d'Armes. However the king had to give way faced with the enormity of the event: accompanied by his family and part of the court, surrounded by a shouting mob, the king set off for Paris. The revolution, which brought about the end of absolute monarchy, destined Versailles to abandonment: the palace of the Sun king returned into the shadows, and in this way Paris had its revenge on the capital of Louis XIV. However, for more than a century Versailles had contributed to the fame of France and her Kings. Proof of this is that today its name unfailingly evokes the memory of absolute monarchy.

This great work with a prestige which is today artistic, spiritual and political, is mainly due to Louis XIV. Versailles was born above all from the creativity of the great king. At the beginning of his reign the small «Château de Courtes» of his father Louis XIII — a hunting pavillion built from 1624 to 1634 by Philibert Le Roy — had already been modified during an initial campaign of work (1622-1665). The fact that Fouquet had recently fallen into disgrace put the team of Vaux le Viscomte at the King's disposal, Le Nôtre, Le Brum, sculptors and specialized workers. From 1668 to 1671 the King started a new campaign of work. The assignment was given to Le Vau.

On the eastern side, the façade in bricks and stone from the ex castle was conserved and beautified and is today the main part of the building which surrounds the Cour de Marbre. The two wings of the ex out building were rised and connected to the castle by new constructions. In the garden, the castle of Louis XIII was confined between three structures built completely of stone.

On the noble floor the central part of this construction was occupied, between two lateral protrusions, by a terrace. This lay out was again once more sightly changed during the 3rd work campaign (1679-1789) undertaken by Jules Hardouin-Mansart.

On the side of the town the new king's architect enlarged the façade with two wings in bricks and stone called «des Ministres». As far as the western façade is concerned, Mansart eliminated the terrace and in its place arranged, between 1687 and 1684, a vast gallery called «Gallery Hall of the Mirrors». From both sides of this central body Mansart built long symmetrical wings called «du Nord» and «du Midi». This is the layout which we can still admire today. The cubic block projecting from the central body is worthy of note. The façade is made rythmic by frontispieces with coupled Ionic columns placed on the rustic base of the ground floor.

Lastly an attic and a balauster decorated with trophies and vases completed the whole. Even though this scene is of an Italian kind of osten-

Castle of Versailles: the entrance gate and partial view of the yard, castle and chapel.

Hall of the war: stucco representing Louis XIV.

tation, it is however tempered by a sober linearity and by a classical equilibrium.

At the same time as this transformation, André Le Nôtre enlarged and restructured the gardens. He took care that this arrangement was in harmony with the castle predisposing the vast arca decorated by «parterres» (flower beds) where the great east-west avenue starts. At the centre there are the two «parterres d'eau» (low rectangular pools) boardered by bronze statues, cast by the Kellers and the work of Coysevox, Tuby, Magnier, Regnaudin, Le Hongre. The avenue which descends towards the grand canal through steps and gentle slopes, goes between the fountains of Diana and the Point du jour and downwards towards the Latona basin, continues on the Tapis Vert which opens into the space which surrounds the Apollo basin on the left and right of the Tapis Vert, the four pools of the «Saisons» are at the intersection of narrowe: avenues, which delimit small woods (in one o these Mansart raised the «colonnade» in 1685) A second avenue from north to south crosse: the first and extends, parallel to the façade o the castle, from the Orangerie — at a lower leve to the parterre du midi, framed by the «de: Cents Marches» steps (the Hundred steps) — t the Neptune basin, decorated under Louis XV by the Slodtzs, by the Adams and b Bouchardon. This vast composition in here to day thanks to long and impressive works of ex cavation and derivation: Le Nôtre has given u:

here the complete model of the French style garden. The decoration and the arrangement were entrusted to Charles Le Brun.

The Magnificent «des Ambassadeurs» flight of steps (1671-1679) led to the large apartments on the noble floor. To the North the king's apartment has essentially maintained its original aspect: coverings of polychrome marbles, ceilings painted with allegories of planets which orbit around the sun, with plaster figures, embossed and gilded bronzes and silver mobiles. To the south the queen's apartment — reached by the marble staircase — was considerably modified in the 18th century.

Between these two apartments the «Grande Galérie» situated between the halls of War and Peace, is decorated with mirrors which amazed the people of the time for their number and size. It is the main hall of the Castle. The vault painted by Le Brun, illustrates the most important moments in the life of the king. The chapel is the last outstanding work. Begun in 1699 following the project of Mansart, and finished in 1710 by Robert de Cotte, it is situated where the north wing begins. It is of the same style as the Palatine Chapel with two floors. An elegant Corinthian fluted colonnade stands above the arch of the nave. This luminous vast space is dominated by the illusory ceiling by Coypel.

The arrangement at the centre of the castle, of the King's Chamber, on the «Cour de Marbre» and the creation of «l'oeil de Boeuf»

Parterre d'eaux. In the foreground the Rhone river.

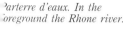

Cour Royale of the Palace of Versailles.

The fountain of Latona.

(the Bull's Eye), which has a gilded plaster frieze representing children's games (1701) goes back to the end of the reign.

This splendid palace was the answer to the King's wish to make Versailles an instrument of government. In this way Louis XIV sheltered the monarchy from the changes of mood of the Parisian mob and united around himself the ministers and administration which underlined the centralization of the government. In addi-

tion he surrounded himself with nobles and by subjecting them he removed any impulse of rebellion on their part.

The luxury of the furnishings, the strict etiquette, the regal magnificence, were all necessary to underline the importance of the seat of power. Louis XIV officially settled into Versailles with his court on 6th May 1682. Versailles on the other hand played an essential role in the economical policy of the King: the castle to which everyone had freedom of access became a kind of permanent exibition of French arts and crafts. The cerimony of court did not pay heed to the intimacy of the sovereigns therefore the king had no other refuge than his private apartments and the trianon. From 1670, in this small estate, Louis XIV had had a building constructed by Le Vau (Le Trianon de Porcelaine) covered with Delft majolica, which in 1687 was substituted by a construction which Mansart was asked to plan: a small palace covered with pink marble spreads its two wings and peristyle along the flower beds full of flowers.

When Louis XIV died on first September 1715, Versailles had already been built along its main lines, as it appears to us on the exterior at the present day. The work of his successors consisted above all in modifying the apartments.

In 1722 the king and his court returned to Versailles which had been abandoned during the regency. The vast Hercules hall, inaugurated

The small wood of the «colonnade».

Fountain with putti (statues of children).

The garden of the oranges and, on the right, the fountain with the Apollo carriage.

in 1736 and decorated by François Lemoyne, conserves a traditional solemnity with its facing of polychrome marble and its ceiling, where however the Apotheosis of the semi-god is of an aerial lightness. But Louis XIV soon chose more intimate and confortable arrangements, which he obtained at the price of demolition such as that of the «des ambassadeurs» steps (1752).

The small apartments of the King on the first floor, and also those of his family, reflect this new frame of mind. The magnificent wall coverings of Jacob Verbeckt and of Jules-Antoine Rousseau show the triumph of the «rocaille»: the king's study, the apartments of M.me Adélaîde, of the Dauphine and the Dauphiness (1747), of the ladies in waitings.

But the most beautiful inheritance of the reign is, without doubt, the Opéra, inaugurated on the

Louis XIV portrayed by Rigaud. On the right, detail of the Great Galerie des Glaces.

The Great Galerie des Glaces.

The Chapel: interiors.

On the right, the room of the King and the room of the Queen.

The Opéra, by the architect A. Gabriel. Below, the Hall of the Battles.

occasion of the marriage of the Dauphin to the Archduchess Marie Antoniette of Austria, wich took place on 16th May 1772. For Jacques-Ange Gabriel, architect and decorator who enjoyed the kings trust, this was his «Canto del Cigno» (Swan Song). The hall with the ligneous wall coverings painted to imitate marble, with the gold and the upper colonnade, the foot lights and the atrium illustrate the return of an architectural style in which the harmony equals the luxury.

In 1750 at Trianon, Gabriel erected the elegant «Pavillon Français»: in 1762 Louis XV had asked him to build a small castle for the Marchioness de Pompadour. This is the small trianon finished in 1768, with a square plan, incomparable for the purity of the design of the four different façades and for the fascination of the ornamental design. It is the first triumph of the «Return to Antiquity».

Louis XVI did not inherit the passion for transformation from his predecessors; the apartments were only partly modernized (the library of Louis XVI - 1774). The queen's chamber, which had already been modified for Maria Leszczynska, was decorated with a magnificent tapestry in silk, woven at Lyon on cartoons by Philippe de Lassalle. Richard Mique arranged with excellent taste, a small apartment for Marie Antoniette («Salon Doré» - 1783). In 1774 Louis XVI gave the small trianon to Marie Antoniette. So the queen had Mique plan an English style garden in which he erected some

buildings (the «Belvédère», the «Temple d l'Amour») then, around the lake, between 178 and 1786, she had him build the «Hameau» (th queen's village consisting of: the «Maison de l Reine», the «Ferme», the «Moulin à eau», th «Laiterie», the «Tour de Marlbourgh»).

The revolutionary storm emptied the castle Napoleon, Louis XVIII and Charles X though of settling there, but could not carry out thei plan. Louis-Philippe secured the castle makin, the Government approve a law which destine the property of Versailles and the Trianon t the civil list.

Every sovreign who lived in Versailles left hi own individual mark there. The enormous com plex of the Palace, the park and the Triano offer inexaustible riches both to the curious an to the historian of art. In 1878 a young provir cial man came to Paris to visit the monument and museums of the capital, and dedicated th last afternoon of his stay to Versailles. The cas tle was then the «Musée d'Histoire» of kin Louis-Philippe dedicated «to all the glories c France».

Notwithstanding the transformations carrie out by the king, the young man was fascinatec The same evening after his visit to the palac of king he noted in his agenda: «the most beau tiful thing there is in Paris is Versailles». Thi young man was Pierre de Nolhac. His nomina tion to the appointment of Guardian of Ver sailles in November 1892, his culture and hi solicitude for this dream palace contributed t the rediscovery of its history.

There is nothing left to do but hope that th numerous visitors who come to Versailles eve ry year understand its meaning and what symbolizes: in this way they will have an ide of the influence which ancient France coul once exert.

The Grand Trianon.

Above: the Petit Trianon and the Temple de l'Amour.

Bust of Marie Antoinette.

The village of Marie Antoinette.

Château de Malmaison: bust of Napoleon.

Château de Malmaison, today seat of a Museum.

Château de Malmaison: «Napoleon crosses the Alps».

Château de Fontainebleau:
comprehensive view.

FONTAINEBLEU

The town of Fontainebleu is proud to have a castle where the kings of France lived, from the Capets to Napoleon III. Its origin is due to the surrounding forests which are rich in game: in the 12th century, the kings, who loved to hunt, established a residence near a spring called «la fontaine de Bliaud».

During the Renaissance, Francis I entrusted Gilles Le Breton with the construction of a complex of buildings to substitute the medieval inhabitance. The main buildings to the north and east of the Cour du Cheval Blanc (courtyard of the White Horse) and the parts to the west and north of the oval courtyard, the «Galérie François I», connect the two courtyards. The castle, which was the favorite home of the king, is decorated with great care by the «École de Fontainebleau», a group of Italian, Flemish and French artists, directed by the Italians, Rosso and Primaticcio. Their most complete work remains the «Galérie François I», decorated between 1534 and 1540. The combination of 12 small frescos framed by stuccoes is an innova-

tion of the School. This complex is an apology, altough in a very enigmatical form of the royal duties. In the ball room, completed under Henry II, the pictorial genius of Primaticcio is united with the architectonical genius of Philibert de l'Orme.

During the reign of Henry IV, the aspect of the castle evolved. The Cour des Offices, the Jeu de Paume and a wing of the Cour des Princes were built and the oval courtyard was completed. The decoration bears the mark of a more French design, elaborated by the second «École de Fontainebleau» where oil paintings harmonize with the painted wooden facings. The vaults of the Trinity chapel were painted by Martin Fréminet.

Under Louis XIII, Jean du Cerceau dignified the White Horse courtyard with the idea of the magnificent «horse shoe» staircase.

In the reign of Louis XV the south wing of the courtyard was built under the direction of Gabriel. The «escalier du Roi» (King's staircase) was built between the walls of a room decorated with stuccoes by Primaticcio. But above all, in the 17th and 18th centuries, work

Entrance gate: detail.

Show-case with the hat of Napoleon I.

Portrait of Napoleon. On the right, details of the Chapel gate and the landscape-park.

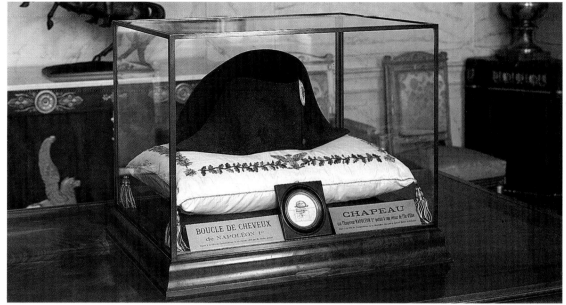

was carried out on the interior arrangement, especially in the apartments called «des Reines Mères et du Pape» (of the Queen Mothers and the Pope»).

Improvements were continued under Napoleon according to the style of the period, such as the furnishing of Josephine's Petits apartments. The Emperor also left a sentimental mark: the White Horse courtyard was renamed «cour des Adieux» after Napoleon's farewell ceremony to his guard (20th April, 1814).

Chambord: the castle seen from above.

CHAMBORD

The castles of the Loire were mostly built between 1418, the year of the escape of the Dauphin Charles VII from Paris, and 1524, the destruction of Pavia followed by the return of Francis I to Paris. Between these two dates the kings of France lived in this beautiful region, renewing or building numerous castles. Many stately homes were also built there because a good courtisan must live near the king.

At the beginning of his reign, Francis I lived in the Castle of Blois with his wife Claudia of France. As he desired to have his own palace, the young king had the most elegant, majestic and fairy-like castle of the Loire built: Chambord. It is at the centre of an enormous forest rich in game at 14 km from Blois. This castle is a masterpiece of the early Renaissance.

At the beginning of the 14th century the Italian artistic influence began to be felt in France. At this time gothic art was submerged and the French Renaissance was born. The Maecenas policy of Francis I, upheld the movement, favouring the aesthetical affermation of the early Renaissance. The castle of Chambord, begun in 1519 at the accession of Henry II, following the model of the other Loire castles, was a fusion between French 15th century architecture and that of the Italian Renaissance. In fact the project is drawn from the medieval French and the gothic is present in the high roofing with sky-lights, in the façades and in the form of the enormous spiral staircase. However the internal arrangement is of Italian inspiration, for example, the great hall with a staircase in the centre, or the distribution of the apartments in the towers. Above all, the decorations which are inspired by Italian art can be seen in the putti, the vine-tendrils, the friezes or the rose windows.

The general idea is inspired by the medieval plans for strongholds in the plains: a rectangular wall, reinforced by barrages protects a keep flanked by 4 round towers. However the innovation is to be found in the keep which is planned centered around the wide staircase.

The spiral staircase. This is a wonder of Chambord and it is an adaption of Italian taste to an element of French tradition. Was it perhaps planned by the Italian Master, Leonardo da Vinci? Its helicoidal spiral ingeniously unfolds a double ramp and it is possible for two processions to pass at the same time without meeting.

The scenary. The Italian richness of the sculpture ends at the roof tops, where it forms a magical harmonious whole: roofs bristling with chimneys, spires and turrets, among which the lantern, 32 m high, appears.

Chambord: the huge stairway.

The house of Claude Monet.

studies is on the ground floor, another is near the greenhouses to the left of the house, and lastly, on the opposite side is the spacious, luminous study called «des nymphéas» (of the nymphs), built in 1916. There Monet painted his artistic testimony, the «Décorations des nymphéas».

The gardens. The real study of the Master was always the garden which he had lovingly planned and looked after himself. Two different ideas brought the creation of the two gardens about: in front of the house is the «Clos Normand» and further away is the acquatic garden.

The Clos Normand. This is a French style garden which includes a fantasy of multitudes of plants. According to the time of year, nasturtiums, narcissis, tulips, azaleas, gladioli, daisies, roses, wisterias, rhododendrons and Japanese cherry trees give their colours to form a splendid whole. The central avenue, covered with arches full of flowers, leads to the house and to the two large yew trees.

The aquatic garden. In 1893, Monet bought some land on the Paris side of Clos Normand. Here he created an exotic garden with luxurious vegetation. Weeping willows shade a pond covered with water lilies and it is crossed by various bridges. One of these, the «pont Japonais», is romantically covered by climbing plants and is famous for having inspired many works of the Master. The different varieties of water lilies gave rise to the main works of Monet: the series of «Nymphéas» and above all his «Decorations de nymphéas», which he painted during the last years of his life, a brilliant conclusion to an exceptional artistic ability.

GIVERNY

The home of Claude Monet. The French artist, Claude Monet (1840-1926), is the greatest representative of impressionism. This trend in painting at the end of the 19th century, which arose in reaction to academic art, tried to represent the transitory aspect of life. Nature and light soon became its main objective. The gardens of Giverny were the «study» used by Monet at the height of his glory, between 1883, the year in which he settled in Giverny and 1926, the year of his death.

The house. The pink of the plastering, the green of the blinds, the balustrade of the terrace and of the arches in the garden, give the house a fascinating impressionist aspect. The garden, closely connected to the façade, mixes its colours with it. Colour reigns in the inside too: two tones of yellow make the dining room sunny while a harmony of blue warms the kitchen. Many prints collected by Monet decorate the whole of the house. One of the artists

On the right, the gardens and the small lake near the «Japanese» bridge. Below, lake and the artist's boat.

Chartres: the cathedral.

The cathedral: the big large-windows.

CHARTRES

The capital of rich Beauce, Chartres was an important commercial centre and agricultural market. It was also the destination of pilgrims as it possessed the Holy Tunic which the Virgin was wearing on the day of the Annunciation, a famous relic given to the town by Charles the Bald (about 875). During the episcopacy of Fulbert, in the 11th century, the intellectual influence of Chartres extended to Europe. The fires of 1145 and 1194 only spared the cript of the glorious Romanesque cathedral, apart from the royal doorway in the western façade and the two towers. The main part of the new cathedral was built between 1194 and 1220, this was in record time and was due to the richness of donations and to the voluntary work of the masons. This gave rise to an almost unique homogeneity of gothic style; besides this, this building marks the starting point of the great art of the 13th century cathedrals.

Description of the Exterior. Romanesque and gothic styles harmonize the façade. To the left, the «clocher neuf» (new bell tower) goes back to the first half of the 12th century. The sober «clocher vieux» (old bell tower) to the right, was built a few years earlier, surmounted by a magnificent gothic spire. The triple royal doorway, a masterpiece of romanesque sculpture, which also comes from the previous church; at the centre is the Advent of the Apocalypse surrounded by scenes from the life of Christ. The column-statues of the early gothic period show a considerable contrast between the stiffness of the bodies and expressiveness of the faces. The rose window and the kings' gallery are of the 13th century.

The apse, harmoniously arranged with steps, is crowned by rampant pointed arches similar to roses, connected to each other by buttresses.

Interior. The nave is exceptionally wide. The elimination of the women's galleries has now reduced the height to only three floors. This innovation had two technical consequences: the possibility of opening larger windows and the more important role of the pointed arches.

The double deambulatorium of the choir and the width of the transept were the answer to the problems created by the pilgrims who poured in continually.

The windows. If today the nave seems dark, it was however very light according to medieval standards. In fact the windows here take up a lot of space, thanks to the elimination of the women's gallery. These openings are decorated with wonderful glass windows of the 12th and 13th centuries. The rose window in the western façade is dedicated to the Last Judgement; the three Romanesque windows below, are still dominated by a bichrome in red and blue, and the people represented there still demonstrate a stately attitude. The transept is illuminated by two rose windows and by other pointed windows.

Index

Alphabetical Index

Editorial and graphic
Federico Frassinetti

The photographic service has been completed by Foto Pix - Paris - Alceo Marino - Federico Frassinetti - Photo Quiresi
Translation into English by Art - Bologna

Printed on chromomat paper by the paper-mill Arjomari - Prioux - France
Dépôt légal 2er trimestre 1988

Printed in April 1988 in the lithographic plant
LA FOTOMETALGRAFICA EMILIANA SPA
San Lazzaro di Savena - Bologna